DOWNFALL:
Secularization
of a
Christian Nation

DOWNFALL:
Secularization
of a
Christian Nation

by
MARTY PAY
and
HAL DONALDSON

New Leaf
Press

FIRST EDITION
1991

Typesetting by: Total Type & Graphics
                   Berryville, AR 72616

Library of Congress Catalog Number:
ISBN: 0-89221-193-8

DEDICATION

To Chuck Colson, James Dobson, and Al Sanders for lighting a fire under me.

To John Stewart for maintaining that flame.

To my best friend, my wife Donna, who loved me and stood by me in the good and not so good times.

—Marty Pay

To "Gram" and Mom—women of compassion and courage.

—Hal Donaldson

ACKNOWLEDGEMENT

One of my greatest joys in writing this book is the platform it provides to thank some special individuals the Lord has used to help me on this journey. Most are persons I have come to know, love, and admire. Admittedly, some will not agree with me or with each other on all issues presented herein. But to some degree they have all influenced my life and this book, and for that I want to thank the following:

Jerry Nordskog, chairman of the Southern California Constitution Education Committee; Greta Coe, co-director of Sanctity of Human Life Ministries; the Reverend Steve Larson, Evangelical Free Church of Conejo Valley; Russ Hauth; Karen McClaine, Darlene Johnson, Sharon Spence, Carol Howel, and Karol Burkhardt; Elizabeth Skogland, author and family counselor; Jane Chastain, board member of Concerned Women of America; Jo Ellen Allen, president of California Eagle Forum; Doc Burch, chaplain for the California Republican Assembly; Father "Jim" Stehly, Saint Paschal Baylon; Lori Hougens, Right to Life League; the Hughes family; Pastor Jim Harris; Pastor George Rutenbar and Bethany Baptist Church, Thousand Oaks; Susie Carpenter McMillan, president, Right to Life; Suzy Carson, former producer of KKLA; Doug and Kathy Kay, California Care Coalition; Sara Hardman, president, San Fernando Valley chapter, California Republican Assembly; Leslie Dutton, president, American Association of Women; Helen Fabian, KBRT; Debbie Quinn, producer of K-LIFE; Vicki Enscoe; Debbie Scott; Eadie Gieb, Parents and Students United; Geri Urrutia, Shield of Roses; Teri Reiser, Right to Life League; La-Vonne Wilenken; Pastor Chris Hoops, American Heritage Church; Earl and Phyllis Wiggin, Home Books; Larry Levenson; Dave Austin, Country Oaks Baptist, Tehachapi; Dave Donaldson, Southern California Director of ChurchCare Network; Karen Johnson, Director, Conejo Valley Crisis Pregnancy Center; Pam Butler; Ted Rohlfsen and Tim Fish; Pastor Dan Schneider, Calvary Chapel, Tehachapi; Terry Donnelly; and my good friend Richard Grant—a strong believer who at one time doubted the depth of our Christian heritage and our place in society. He made me realize that this book must be written so Believers could see how the *Secularization of a Christian Nation* occurred.

—Marty Pay

ACKNOWLEDGEMENT

My deepest appreciation to Marty Pay, who has been used by God to awaken many to the attack against our Creator and Judeo-Christian values in America.

Studies have shown that 80 percent of the college students in America consider religion important in their lives, and more than 50 percent occasionally read the Bible and attend worship services. Another survey showed that 94 percent of Americans believe in God or a universal spirit. These and other statistics led a well-known pollster to conclude, "In 50 years, the nation's social order has undergone rapid and profound transformations with little effect on measures of personal faith.... Basic religious beliefs, and even religious practice, today differ relatively little from the levels recorded 50 years ago."

Many have generally concurred with this pollster's conclusion. But this book defies the polls and those who would misconstrue their meaning. Polls, it should be noted, can be misleading, for they do not account for society's rapidly changing perception of "religiosity." Clearly, despite the polls and "expert" interpretations, the role of religion in American society **has** changed. The information compiled herein is too overwhelming to discount.

Downfall: Secularization of a Christian Nation is revealing, thought-provoking and disturbing. Thank you, Marty, for having the courage and foresight to write such a book.

Heartfelt thanks to Doree Donaldson, Ken Horn, Daryl Perna, and Virgina Allen.

—Hal Donaldson

FOREWORD

America began its experiment in self-government founded upon the Judeo-Christian ethic. Our founding fathers affirmed this foundation and through the educational system, passed it on to succeeding generations. Students trained in this tradition affirmed this ideal when they matured and became leaders in the arts, religion, business, education, and in the governmental process.

Horace Mann and John Dewey were leaders in changing how we Americans educate the next generation. Dewey was an original signer of the Humanist Manifesto in 1933. This document is in stark contrast to the Judeo-Christian ethic by asserting there is no God.

Up until this time, the Cultural War between these conflicting philosophies was always present in America but the forces of Secular Humanism were on the outside looking in, seeking acceptance.

Since 1933, the tide has been moving in the opposite direction and our society has now produced leaders in the arts, religion, business, education, and in the governmental process, not limited to the courts, who either affirm Secular Humanism as the religion of America, or if willing to affirm the Judeo-Christian ethic as the foundation of our society, prefer to do so in private for fear that a public affirmation of its principles might make someone uncomfortable.

Marty Pay and Hal Donaldson accurately describe this entire process with astute clarity and a clear vision of what is needed to correct it. If we Americans wonder why we are wallowing in drugs, abortion, crime, homosexuality, marital instability, and a growing economic crisis, this focus on the Cultural War which has gripped America is must reading. A spiritual crisis is rampant in America and those of us who prefer the Judeo-Christian ethic have the duty to lead the way to affirm that there are fixed standards and moral absolutes which God gave to man by which he is to live.

Fullerton, California
October, 1990

We Americans believe and accept that it is not the function of government, federal or state, to establish a state religion. We believe that God has given man certain rules to live by—contained in the Bible—and that voters and holders of public office are to supplement these principles in deciding moral issues in the kingdom of man.

To this end, I suggest the following actions for concerned citizens:

1. Register to vote—decide for yourself which political party or candidate is led by the philosophy of the Judeo-Christian ethic and which are led by the philosophy of Secular Humanism.

2. Be informed—study candidates for school board, city, county, state, and federal office to determine what beliefs motivate them, and whether they will follow God's law in supplementing public policy decisions.

3. Get involved—join a civic organization to help affirm and build influence for Judeo-Christian principles.

Some of these groups include Christian Voters League, American Family Association, Traditional Values Coalition, Concerned Women for American, Eagle Forum, and various pro-life organizations.

Some people express concern that the kingdom of man is hopeless and that attempts to save it are fruitless. I beg to differ. We all must live with the kingdom of man until He whose right it is to reign returns to take His proper place among us. Government and the exercise of our religious beliefs are entwined. We must protect our rights and must help to create a better or tolerable environment in which to raise our children.

—William E. Dannemeyer
Member of Congress

This could be the most valuable book on American history you will ever read. Thanks Marty Pay and Hal Donaldson for giving us the foundation to springboard into the kind of future our founding fathers intended.

—Jane Chastain
Broadcaster, author

This timely book should be read by every Christian concerned about the state of our culture.

—Dr. Theodore Baehr
Chairman/CEO
Good News Communications

The retreat from America's Judeo-Christian heritage as described in this book should spur every Christian to citizen action. Their childrens' future demands it.

—Dr. Jo Ellen Allen
President, California
Eagle Forum

CONTENTS

INTRODUCTION

When Darwin introduced his Theory of Evolution, he evoked cries of heresy and blasphemy. But, in time, the theory gained more acceptance within the scientific community—so much so, that by the 1920s the theory had meandered its way into the American classroom. What ensued was a verbal war between two strong-willed factions: Bible-believing Christians and professing Darwinians.

The inflammatory debate came to a head in July, 1925 with the Scopes Trial. John T. Scopes, a high school science teacher, had been arrested for violating Tennessee's Anti-Evolution Law. He had been charged with using a textbook which taught that man descended from apes. Groups with a vested interest converged on Dayton, Tennessee with the revelry of delegates attending a political convention. The American Civil Liberties Union attained the services of high-powered attorney Clarence Darrow and others to serve in Scope's defense. William

Jennings Bryan, a former presidential candidate and Secretary of State, led a team of prosecuting attorneys.

As the proceedings commenced in the Rhea County Courthouse, with one thousand persons packed into a room which had a seating capacity of seven hundred, it was obvious that this was more than just another case. A huge banner hanging over the courtyard proclaimed, "Read Your Bible Daily for One Week." Revival tents were set up on the outskirts of town. Fundamentalist ministers throughout the South had descended on this small community to make certain their convictions were known. The courtroom was sprinkled with jeers and "amens." But the stakes were too high to allow the carnival atmosphere to sway the court's decision. The trial of one teacher had, in essence, become the arena to determine the beginning of man, the existence of God, and the role religion would play in the nation's future.

Americans waited impatiently for the verdict.

In a sense, decades later, we are still waiting. The battle to determine religion's place in society is still being waged between Christians and secularists.

Unfortunately, many Christians have chosen to shield their eyes to the dispute at hand. I must confess that at one time I too was one who shrugged his civic responsibility. I dodged petition tables and ignored pleas to become involved in efforts to combat such offenses as abortion and pornography. I seriously questioned whether Christians could have a positive influence on our system. I had my doubts whether Christians could turn back the tide of secularism in our society: "So why make the effort?" I often asked myself.

After reading Chuck Colson's bestselling book *Kingdom's in Conflict* and listening to him field calls on the radio, I began to realize what occurs when Christians do not become involved. Colson said secularism advances as orthodoxy retreats. I fell to my knees shortly after reading his book and began seeking God's forgiveness. I finally understood that by being silent and civically slothful, I was aiding those who were aiming to secularize this nation. It was apparent that I had an obligation to God to become involved in the civic arena, to work to uphold the values this nation was founded upon.

Speaking to a group of Christians about a year later, I passed out a questionnaire dealing with a variety of issues: abortion, pornography, euthanasia, and more. It was astonishing to read the responses from members of the group. Their answers were not based on biblical understanding, but rather reflected the extent to which they had been secularized. These "Bible-believing" individuals had been taught to think secularly, and thus, their Christian convictions had been virtually relegated from their decision making process. They had, subconsciously, assimilated the humanistic concepts of relativity which tear at the fabric of biblical absolutes. Perhaps watching television four hours a day versus studying the Bible two hours a week accounted, in part, for their tainted values.

Because a large percentage of our society (including many Christians) has fallen prey to secularism, one must ask whether this is indeed a Christian nation. Certainly our once well-founded Judeo-Christian consensus has been altered. Our political and educational systems, entertainment and news gathering industries, nuclear families, and mainstream churches wear the stains of secularism.

Paul Vitz, noted educator and author, pointed to our secularized educational system as a key factor in this spiritual decay. What is not taught becomes insignificant, he claimed. Because Christianity's contributions to society have been left out of school curricula and biblical principles are being ignored in the classroom and at home, Vitz believes humanism has filled the void with its ungodly ideals.

To reverse this trend and return to the values our nation was founded upon, Christians must return to their rightful place as vigorous participants in the civic arena.

A priest was walking beside me in a march at Universal Studios. An estimated 25,000 believers were on hand to protest the showing of the film *The Last Temptation of Christ*. I noted, "You must have strong feelings about this film."

He glanced up at me and said, "I do. This is where I'm supposed to be; this is something I have to do."

I understood what he was inferring. Civic activism, to some degree—whether it be voting, praying, or marching—must be incumbent on every Christian if we are to restore America to its godly roots.

In the throes of World War II my grandparents were living in Holland. One afternoon my grandmother saw a truckload of Nazis stop at a cafe. The uniformed men jumped out of the bed of the truck brandishing machine guns. At random, they collected a group of men and boys and placed them in a row; then they shot them to death in retaliation for the assassination of a German official by members of the "underground."

Shortly thereafter, my grandparents took my mother to an "underground" meeting held in an air-raid shelter. There they showed her the coffins of others who had been murdered by Hitler's soldiers. "We want you to see this so you will not forget what has happened."

Driving home one evening in November, 1987, it dawned on me that many in our society—Christians and non- Christians alike—**have** forgotten what has happened **here**. They have forgotten our heritage, that this was once a nation based on the Bible, that it had a Christian consensus. They have failed to recognize the blatant signs which reveal the extent to which America has been secularized. This book is an attempt to retrace America's steps from its founding to the heels of the twenty-first century, to illustrate in a concise historical fashion the decisions, persons, and events which have led this nation to the brink of becoming a secularized state. Moreover, this is a literary plea intended to stir believers to action—to work toward reversing this tide of secularism in America.

Every student of history confronts the temptation of sensationalizing history—that is to cross the line of objectivity by coloring the facts to support a particular perspective. This book is not based on fiction or embellished history. Admittedly, however, this book does represent my bias. But, after all, most historical reporters do have philosophies or opinions based on their interpretation of history. William S. Kilborne, Jr., in *Etc. Journal*, referred to this bias when he said, "Historians are abstractors: They first abstract a topic; they then abstract from a vast array of primary materials those they choose to pay attention to; they then abstract from those materials they have chosen to pay attention to, those materials which they will include in their history. Each of these choices reflects a personal preference, or, if you will, a bias."

The mere title, *Downfall: Secularization of a Christian Nation*, represents my bias. I believe America has become secularized... to the point that it risks destruction. We are flirting with disaster. In order to rescue America, to alter her course, it is imperative that we understand which decisions and philosophies have led to this demise.

In March, 1989, Supreme Court Justice Sandra Day O'Connor was widely lambasted for claiming that the high court had endorsed the notion that "this is a Christian nation." She cited three cases where this was addressed by the court. In 1892, the court said, "This is a Christian nation." In 1952, Justice William O'Douglas wrote, "We are a religious people whose institutions presuppose a Supreme Being." In 1961, Justice Felix Frankfurter penned, "Religious beliefs pervade, and religious institutions have traditionally regulated, virtually all human life."

Nonetheless, media personalities, law professors and activists condemned O'Connor's statement. If her comment had been made at the time of the founding of this nation, it would not have evoked **one** vehement response. For we were once a Christian nation. Are we now?

Noah Webster's *American Dictionary of the English Language,* published in 1828, defines **secular:** "pertaining to the present world, or things not spiritual or holy." Webster's *Pocket Dictionary*, published by Harper and Row in 1962 defines **secular:** "worldly; non-spiritual."

In 1828, Webster defined the word **Christian:** "a believer in the religion of Christ; ... a real disciple of Christ; one who believes in the truth of the Christian religion, and studies to follow the example, and obeys the precepts, of Christ."

According to these definitions, is America secular or Christian? The following pages will help readers reach an opinion and, ideally, awaken a slumbering people to action.

—Marty Pay

ONE

THE FOUNDING: IN GOD WE TRUSTED

> Our constitution was made only for a moral and
> religious people. It is wholly inadequate for the
> government of any other.
> —John Adams

In the nineteenth century, the U.S. Government began stamping "In God We Trust" on its coins; the phrase represented the nation's commitment to the Almighty.

America was founded by a people with an unyielding determination to worship God. They found solace in the knowledge that a Supreme Being was guiding their footsteps, protecting, and providing. The consensus in Colonial America was based on the Judeo-Christian ethic. Children prayed in the classroom, churches were reverenced, and the Bible was revered. This fact must be understood and accepted before one can adequately comprehend the extent to which America has been secularized.

THE MAYFLOWER MISSION

The Mayflower was one of many ships from Europe destined for America which challenged the turbulent Atlantic in the early 1600s. But this particular voyage was unusual because the vessel was carrying a band of religious outcasts who were seeking the freedom to worship their God without governmental interference.

Noted historians Charles and Mary Beard confirmed the travelers' intentions:

> The motives provoking men and women to brave the perils of the sea voyage in slow sailing vessels overcrowded with passengers and to risk their lives and fortunes in a strange continent, far from their native habitats, were no doubt various. But historical records justify such a summary as follows: ....An eagerness to escape religious persecutions and to found communities in which they could worship God in their own ways, free from the domination of church and government officials trying to enforce conformity to other faiths.

This religious group reiterated its faith and purpose while anchored off the New England coast in 1620; they composed what would become known as the Mayflower Compact:

> In the name of God, Amen. We whose names are underwritten, the loyal subjects of our dread sovereign Lord, Kings James, by the grace of God, of Great Britain, France and Ireland, King, defender of the faith, having undertaken, for the glory of God and advancement of the Christian

faith, and honor of our king and country, a voyage
to plant the first colony in the Northern parts of
Virginia, do by these solemnly and mutually in
the presence of God, and one another, covenant
and combine ourselves together into a civil body
politic, for our better ordering and preservation
and furtherance of the ends aforesaid....

FAITH IN THE COLONIES

As immigrants settled in America, they brought with
them deep religious convictions. Most were Protestants
who had grown disenchanted with England's oppression. Though Colonialists of the Quaker, Baptist, Presbyterian, and Lutheran faiths had their theological differences, they were united in the quest for religious freedom.
The Beards wrote, "...religious considerations entered
into the founding and development of every colony from
New Hampshire to Georgia."

While speaking before Britain's Parliament in 1775 to
propose resolutions of conciliation with the colonies in
America, Sir Edmund Burke said:

Their governments are popular in an high
degree...and this share of the people in their ordi-
nary government never fails to inspire them....
Religion, always a principle of energy, in this new
people is no way worn out or impaired; and their
mode of professing it is also one main cause of this
free spirit. The people are Protestants, and of that
kind which is the most adverse to all implicit
submission of mind and opinion. This is persuasion not only favorable to liberty, but built upon
it.... All Protestantism, even the most cold and

passive, is a sort of dissent. But the religion most prevalent in our northern colonies is a refinement of the principle of resistance: it is the dissidence of dissent, and the protestantism of the Protestant religion.[1]

Because the majority of colonialists were Protestant, other faiths, namely Catholicism, were not always tolerated. To avoid religious infighting, however, colonies such as Maryland passed laws which would grant freedom of worship to anyone professing "faith in Jesus Christ."

Most respected historians agree: The consensus in Colonial America was based on a belief in God and the Judeo-Christian ethic.

IN THE BEGINNING

Before the founding fathers penned the governing documents endeared by America, their philosophies were being shaped by the writings of Christian men like John Locke, Baron Montesquieu, and William Blackstone.

Locke, a seventeenth century democratic theorist in England, had a profound influence on the patriots of the American Revolution. His works—"Essay Concerning Human Understanding," "The Reasonableness of Christianity," and "Two Treatises on Government"—were foundational to the principles upon which this nation was established. His words were quoted in speeches and treaties, and used extensively in the Declaration of Independence. Locke developed many of his precepts from Scripture. He was known for his public declarations concerning the goodness of God and the importance of studying the Bible.

Montesquieu's gift to American democratic life came, to a large extent, from his work, "The Spirit of Law"—a set of guidelines for establishing a free society among men who possess a **sinful nature**. The work discussed the branches of government, separation of powers, representation, and a system of checks and balances. The Frenchman based his blueprint for a democratic society on faith in the Almighty. Montesquieu said:

> God is related to the universe, as Creator and Preserver; the laws by which He created all things are those by which He preserves them. He acts according to these rules, because He knows them; He knows them because He made them; and He made them, because they are in relation to his wisdom and power....

Blackstone was revered for his studies of law, today known as "Blackstone's Commentaries." His supposition—that the Supreme Being's law was superior to man's and therefore He is the bestower of human rights—found its way into the Declaration of Independence:

> We hold these truths to be self-evident, that all men are created equal, that they are endowed by their Creator with certain unalienable rights...that among these are life, liberty and the pursuit of happiness.

Blackstone wrote:

> ....when the Supreme Being formed the universe, and created matter out of nothing, He impressed certain principles upon that matter, from which it

can never depart, and without which it would cease to be. When He put the matter into motion, He established certain laws of motion, to which all movable bodies must conform.

DECLARATION OF INDEPENDENCE

June 11, 1776 a committee was formed to draft the Declaration of Independence. The committee consisted of Thomas Jefferson, Benjamin Franklin, John Adams, Roger Sherman, and Robert Livingston. From the group, Jefferson was elected to compose a first draft. With extensive input from Adams and Franklin, Jefferson made at least sixteen revisions before submitting it to the Continental Congress for alterations and approval.

The Judeo-Christian tradition—principles espoused by Locke, Montesquieu, and Blackstone—permeate the Declaration of Independence. Equality: "We hold these truths to be self-evident that all men are created equal...;" God-given rights: "laws of nature and nature's God;" self-government: "Governments are instituted among men, deriving their just powers from the consent of the governed."

CONNECTICUT AND THE U.S. CONSTITUTION

January 14, 1639, as a basis for the government of three towns, the Fundamental Orders of Connecticut were composed. The preamble of the set of laws stated:

Forasmuch as it has pleased the Almighty God by the wise disposition of his divine prudence so to order and dispose of things that we the inhabitants and residents of Windsor, Hartford and

Wethersfield are now cohabiting and dwelling in and upon the River Connecticut and the lands thereunto adjoining; and well knowing where a people gathered together the Word of God requires that to maintain peace and union of such a people there should be an orderly and decent government established according to God, to order and dispose of the affairs of the people....

The Orders of Connecticut became a model for other state constitutions, including, the U.S. Constitution—adopted a century later.

In May, 1787, at Independence Hall in Philadelphia, many of the Constitutional Convention delegates were voicing their displeasures and concerns. Slavery, equal representation, and limitations on the federal government's control of states were issues which threatened to divide the delegation, if not the country.

In the midst of vociferous chaos, eighty-one-year-old Benjamin Franklin stood to his feet. A hush came to the room as he called for daily prayers to be conducted at the Convention. He then proceeded to make his now famous speech:

> I have lived, Sir, a long time, and the longer I live, the more convincing proofs I see of this truth—that God governs in the affairs of men....And if a sparrow cannot fall to the ground without his notice, is it probable that an empire can rise without his aid? We have been assured, Sir, in the sacred writings, that 'except the Lord build the House they labour in vain that build it.' I firmly believe this; and I also believe that without his concurring aid we shall succeed in this political

27

building no better, than the builders of Babel.

The majority of the framers of the Constitution were professing Christians. Most of them had been educated in Christian schools and were well-versed in Scripture. The precious governing document they composed was greatly influenced by their religious persuasions, specifically, the Calvinistic belief that man is basically depraved and prone to sinful indulgences. For that reason, some have dubbed the law of the land "Calvin's Constitution."

THE FEDERALIST PAPERS

Alexander Hamilton was the principal author of the Federalist Papers, though James Madison and John Jay were also responsible for writing some of the essays. The works were published in newspapers throughout the colonies and were successful in rallying grassroots support for the ratification of the Constitution. James Madison wrote in essay 37:

It is impossible for the man of pious reflection not to perceive in it [the Constitution] a finger of that Almighty hand which has been so frequently and signally extended to our relief in the critical states of the revolution.

Hamilton openly confessed his faith in God, having been raised in a Calvinist family. In fact, shortly before his sudden death at the hand of Aaron Burr, he was laying plans to establish the "Christian Constitutional Society"—an organization that would preserve constitutional law and the Christian religion.

Jay, the first chief justice of the Supreme Court, said:

In forming and settling my belief relative to the doctrines of Christianity, I adopted no articles from creeds but such only as, on careful examination, I found to be confirmed by the Bible.... At a party in Paris, once, the question fell on religious matters. In the course of it, one of them asked me if I believed in Christ? I answered that I did, and that I thanked God that I did.

Jay, Madison, and Hamilton campaigned for the ratification of the U.S. Constitution because they believed the document was divinely orchestrated, and just as importantly, it was reflective of their religious convictions.

FOUNDING FATHERS: MEN OF FAITH

There can be no doubt that the founding fathers based their quest for independence on a belief in God and the Scriptures.

Patrick Henry, widely revered for his charismatic speeches, held a deep faith in Jesus Christ. On his death bed he said:

Doctor, I wish you to observe how real and beneficial the religion of Christ is to a man about to die. This is all the inheritance I can give to my dear family. The religion of Christ can give them one which can make them rich indeed. Here is a Book worth more than all others ever printed; yet it is my misfortune never to have read it with proper attention and feeling till lately. I am, however, much consoled by reflecting that the religion of Christ has, from its first appearance in the world, been attacked in vain by all the wits, philosophers, and wise ones, aided by every power of man, and its triumphs have been complete.

John Adams, who succeeded George Washington as president, also had a strong faith in God as evidenced by this letter sent to his son:

My custom is, to read four to five chapters every morning immediately after rising from my bed. It employs about an hour of my time. It is essential, my son, in order that you may go through life with comfort to yourself, and usefulness to your fellow-creatures, that you should form and adopt certain rules or principles, for the government of your own conduct and temper....It is in the Bible, you must learn them, and from the Bible how to practice them. Those duties are to God, to your fellow-creatures and to yourself. 'Thou shalt love the Lord thy God, with all thy heart, and with all thy soul... mind... and strength, and thy neighbor as thyself.'

John Eidsmoe, in his book *Christianity and the Constitution*, said of John Witherspoon, he "is best described as the man who shaped America. Although he did not attend the Constitutional Convention, his influence was multiplied many times over by those who spoke as well as by what was said." The son of a preacher, Witherspoon pastored and later became a college president. He is best known for his civic activism and sermons for the cause of liberty. In 1776, he declared from his pulpit, "He is the best friend of American liberty who is most sincere and active in promoting true and undefiled religion and who sets himself with the greatest firmness to bear down profanity and immorality of every kind."

Perhaps no president in the nation's history has spoken so frequently and eloquently of his dependence on God than George Washington. At his first inaugural address he said:

> ...it would be peculiarly improper to omit in this first official act my fervent supplications to that Almighty Being who rules over the universe, who presides in the councils of nations, and whose providential aids can supply every human defect, that His benediction may consecrate to the liberties and happiness of the people of the United States a Government instituted by themselves for these essential purposes...In tendering this homage to the Great Author of every public and private good, I assure myself that it expresses your sentiments not less than my own, nor those of my fellow-citizens at large... No people can be bound to acknowledge and adore the Invisible Hand which conducts the affairs of men more than those of the United States.

Washington believed in the power of prayer, as evidenced by a twenty-four page booklet of prayers he had written. The following excerpts express his devotion to Jesus Christ:

> O most Glorious God, in Jesus Christ my merciful and loving Father, I acknowledge and confess my guilt, in the weak and imperfect performance of the duties of this day. I have called on Thee for pardon and forgiveness of sins.... Let me live according to those holy rules which Thou hast this

day prescribed in Thy holy word; make me to know what is acceptable in Thy sight....

....Bless the people of this land, be a Father to the fatherless, a Comforter to the comfortless, a Deliverer to the captives, and a Physician to the sick. Let Thy blessings be upon our friends, kindred and families. Be our Guide this day and forever....

At his farewell address, Washington said:

Of all the dispositions and habits which lead to political prosperity, religion and morality are indispensable supports.... Let us with caution indulge the supposition that morality can be maintained without religion.... Reason and experience both forbid us to expect national morality can prevail in exclusion of religious principle.

America's foundation was the Judeo-Christian ethic; her people relied on the Holy Scriptures for moral guidance and civil order, and her leaders relied on them for legislative decisions.

Then the foundation began to crumble.

TWO

FRENCH REVOLUTION: IN MAN THEY TRUSTED

First be atheists, then you will be revolutionaries.
— Victor Jaclard, France, 1868

The ingression of secularistic thought to America can be traced to the mid-1700s when Europe's philosophers began exporting their anti-God ideology. But not until the waning years of the French Revolution—some years later—did these ideals gain nominal acceptance in America's academic circles. What followed was a gradual erosion of the Judeo-Christian consensus in America.

LIFE BEFORE THE REVOLUTION

As France entered the 1780s, she was one of the most powerful countries in Europe. Nevertheless, this feudalistic society was unstable. Two percent of the population—the aristocrats—dominated a struggling middle class, and peasants received few privileges. This volatile climate was fueled by an inadequate, inferior political system: a monarchy which offered little, if any, hope to the downtrodden classes. The absence of a constitution which bestowed equal rights to the common people of France certainly compounded public distrust and disharmony. Kings and landowners lived luxuriously; the serfs, meanwhile, slaved in the fields without opportunity of owning land, of climbing their way to a better life. Eventually, impatience among the rural masses would lead to bloodshed and revolution.

Philosophers—seizing the opportunity—capitalized on the plight of the uprising masses to further their own cause: the spread of secularism. They preached that the French must shed their traditional-religious beliefs and political system before they would find honor, happiness, and liberty. And many believed them.

FATHERS OF SECULARISM

Anti-Christian writers and "free thinkers" abounded in France in the decades preceding the revolution. The degree to which they triggered the violence of the revolt has been debated, but few would dispute that their liberal philosophies became the adopted ideology of many French revolutionaries. In fact, these ideologies provided to many the moral license for revolution and bloodshed.

Voltaire, contrary to his contemporary Montesquieu,

was a French philosopher who devoted much of his energies to denouncing religious tradition. Verna M. Hall, author of *The Christian History of the Constitution*, said:

> Voltaire was undoubtedly a man of rare genius and unequaled skill when it came to the work of destruction. To demolish ancient things was the task in which he excelled and which he delighted to perform. His bitterness against the social system of which the church was an integral part displayed itself with the venom of personal enmity: it was flavored with the passion of revenge rather than a desire to promote right and to prevent wrong.

The influential writer-philosopher Voltaire summed up his hatred for religion when he said, "It took twelve men to establish Christianity; I will show the world that it will take but one man to destroy it."

Rousseau, like Voltaire, became a guru of sorts to many of his French revolutionaries. He established himself "as the model of virtue in a corrupt world and judging all others according to their actions in relation to his virtuous self," said Dena Goodman in her review of Carol Blum's *Rousseau and the Republic of Virtue*. It was France's "'moral bankrupcy' that gave Rousseau moral authority among the revolutionaries. These men... adopted him as 'a model for conceptualizing the self and shaping an ideal state, and as a vehicle for discharging rancor while enhancing self-esteem.'" In essence, Rousseau became more than a hero or a leader. For many, he supplanted the Almighty and his words became as Scripture.

In 1789, the Cercle Social—a group propagating radical and social ideals—surfaced in France. The group functioned under the leadership of Nicolas Bonneville and Claude Fauchet. Both men were well-versed in secularistic ideology. "Immediately after the king's flight, the Cercle Social, through its clubs and its journal, became a major force in a drive to abolish the monarchy and establish a republic which culminated in the mass demonstration and petition signing...," reported Darline Levy in her review of Gary Kates' book *The Cercle Social, the Girondins, and the French Revolution*. The club was prominent in the development of political language and programs "which radicalized large numbers of citizens,...eroding their faith in the legitimacy of constitutional monarchy." The group also fostered the strong anti-church sentiment, which eventually led to an upheaval of the church in France.

THE CHURCH IN FRANCE

To a large degree, the Catholic church was **the** denomination of France, and thereby enjoyed unique privileges. France's Assembly of Clergy—comprised of Catholic bishops and other high ranking church officials— wielded much influence over the government. Prior to the revolution, the government enforced payment of tithe and opted to exempt the church from some taxation. Conversely, up until the dawn of the revolution, Protestants suffered heavy taxation, persecution, imprisonment, and in a few instances, martyrdom.

Radical writers, such as Voltaire, publicly denigrated the state-church for having so much when so many citizens of France were suffering. He said, "A monk— what does he do for a living? Nothing, except to bind himself by an inviolable oath to be a slave and a fool and to live at the expense of other people."

John McManners, in *The French Revolution and the Church*, wrote:

> The philosophers did not inspire the widespread criticism of the monks or the envy of their property, but they organized the mass of individual envies and grievances into a theoretical attack upon the whole concept of the cloistered life and the perpetual vows that were its foundation.

The Jesuit Order in France in 1762 had already been suppressed. The Assembly of Clergy feared other church orders would experience the same fate if outspoken radical philosophers had their way.

Following the first wave of revolution in the 1790s, the church in France began to succumb to the philosopher-perpetuated Age of Enlightenment. The church—corrupt as it was—began to self-destruct under the pressures of a changing political and spiritual climate. The church began to experience dissension within its ranks over such issues as the disparity of privileges and equal representation among diocese. A class system within the clergy had also evolved, ranging from aristocratic priests to "men of the cloth" who belonged to lower classes. These social differences among clergymen led to a diversity of values and opinions on the social issues confronting France. "It was in the church," said Simon Schama, author of *Citizens: A Chronicle of the French Revolution,* "more than any other group in France, that the separation between rich and poor was most bitterly articulated. At stake was not some abstractly defined principle of social justice or natural rights—but the fate of the Christian mission itself."

While church leaders were at each other's "cleric-covered" throats, gradually the church's wealth was siphoned, tithe policies abolished, and church property placed at the disposal of the nation. Though officially these acts were meant to wipe out a government deficit, they were primarily motivated by a shift in national ideology.

The church did not die; however, its influence in the government was virtually eradicated by 1800. No longer were churches reverenced and church leaders endeared by a majority of the populace. Belief in God was not entirely deserted, though Jesus Christ began to be perceived as "a fine teacher" rather than the Son of God and the need for salvation became secondary to the search for happiness. Secular philosophies became the new gospel.

With the church relegated to Sabbath worship centers and church officials "demoted" to worship leaders, the new order of secularism spread like a disease. McManners said, "Enlightened self-interest [Secular Humanism] was the well-spring of moral conduct, and toleration was the first of all virtues. These beliefs constituted the Enlightenment's new doctrine of humanity."

STORMING THE BASTILLE

The Bastille was built in Paris for military use in 1370. The edifice, with its walls eighty feet high, became a prison facility in the 1620s. Struggling classes and radicals despised the prison because they assumed fellow-countrymen were being incarcerated there unfairly. It became a symbol of oppression.

With France's economy near collapse and the price of bread escalating, the common man took to the streets in protest. On July 14, 1789, a mob stormed the Bastille. When the crowd refused to retreat, the guards opened fire. But that merely spawned more violence. Finally, the prison commandant promised to surrender if no danger would come to him and his men. The protesters agreed. But as the guards were withdrawing from the facility they were attacked. The commandant's head was marched through the streets on the end of a pike as if it were a banner of defiance. The crowd commenced to tear down the Bastille stone by stone; in effect, it signified the beginning of the collapse of the monarchy.

The storming of the Bastille was, in part, instigated by Marquis de Sade, an anti-Christian essayist who had been jailed at his mother-in-law's request. From the window of his cell, he urged citizens to liberate him and other "innocent" prisoners. The easily-provoked crowd obliged, only to find "two fools, four forgers and a debaucher" held captive.

As the French government made a habit of succumbing to the riotous demands of boistrous radicals, the monarchy lost whatever respect it held among the citizenry. Eventually feudalism was abolished and a constitution adopted called "The Declaration of the Rights of Man."

In 1792, the monarchy was overthrown and a year later King Louis XVI and his wife Marie Antoinette were executed under the blade of a guillotine. That was the beginning of mass executions. Thousands died. The violence of the next two years mirrored what had occurred at the Bastille. During an eight week period in 1793, fifteen hundred persons were beheaded.

EXPORTING THE REVOLUTION

In *National Review Magazine*, Norman Gash wrote:

[The] civilizing mission of France was assisted, initially perhaps inspired, by the international outlook of the revolution. Formulated by doctrinaires, its ideas were held to be universally valid. Truth was absolute and indivisible. The Revolution was not soley for the benefit of the French people; it was a step forward for all mankind. Revolution therefore was an article for export.[1]

Schama, so aptly said, "From the first year... violence was not just an unfortunate side effect from which enlightened patriots could selectively avert their eyes; it was the revolution's source of collective energy. It was what made the revolution revolutionary." The violent nature of France's revolution—spoken of by Schama—spread throughout Europe in the nineteenth century.
Gash added:

To France's neighbors it was as though a great nation had gone mad; but what is now tragically obvious is that it foreshadowed the Europe of the future. In the century that followed, the explosive mixture of liberalism and nationalism produced revolutions or attempts at revolutions in state after state of continental Europe.... Though in a larger sense the... Revolution was a product of European society, it also helped to shape that society. It did so in two notable ways. The first was what might be called its missionary role. At first by example and then by occupation and annexation, revolutionary France spread its ideas into a large area of Western Europe. As nineteenth century French historians were perhaps too fond of saying, it was the historic destiny of France to bring the enlightened concepts of liberty, equality and fraternity to backward, semi-feudal Europe. Liberalism and reform marched behind French bayonets.[2]

REACTIONS IN THE UNITED STATES

As a gesture of friendship and a symbol of victory for the French revolutionaries, Marquis de Lafayette asked Englishman Tom Paine to deliver keys to the Bastille to George Washington. Schama, in his book, suggested that Washington was not pleased with the "antics of the impetuous and inconsistent French." Washington and other high ranking officials, categorically, refrained from making public statements on the revolution taking place abroad. Some scholars have declared the United States remained neutral because the French had provided financial assistance to the American Revolution.

During one speech, however, Washington did warn against the dispensing of religion as the French were attempting to do. Washington recognized the danger of sending American students abroad, to de-Christianized nations such as France:

It is with indescribable regret, that I have seen the youth of the United States migrating to foreign countries, in order to acquire the higher erudition.... Although it would be injustice to pronounce the certainty of their imbibing maxims not congenial with republicanism, it must nevertheless be admitted, that a serious danger is encountered by sending abroad among other political systems those who have not well learned the value of their own.

Clergymen in America were not reserved in their denunciation of the French and their secularistic philosophies. The Reverend Jedidiah Morse said in 1798:

I am not ashamed now to acknowledge—and thousands have done the same—that this esteem, gratitude, and joy, were the offspring of ignorance. A development of the motives and designs of France, in respect to her alliance and intercourse with us, and of the real nature and object of her revolution, has produced an entire change in my own feelings and opinions. I can no longer consider her government, at any period...as having been truly friendly to the interests of the United States; nor can I believe that the liberty and happiness of Frenchmen, much less those of other nations, were the real objects of a majority of the authors and promoters of her revolution.... Some ...yet cherish an affection which has hitherto served France as a conductor of poisons baneful to our political constitution, to our religion and morals....

Famed nineteenth century educator Emma Willard cast her own aspersions at France:

A nation cannot exist without religion. France tried that and failed. We were born a Protestant Christian nation, and, as such, baptized in blood.... In the conduct of France, too, though gratitude rises in our hearts for her actual services, yet history compelled, though sometimes sorrowfully, to follow truth, must pronounce that in her conduct as a nation, there is nothing virtuous or generous.

A FRENCHMAN VISITS AMERICA

In 1831, French scholar Alexis de Tocqueville returned from a tour of America. He said:

On my arrival in the United States the religious aspect of the country was the first thing that struck my attention; and the longer I stayed there, the more I perceived the great political consequences resulting from this new state of things. In France I had almost always seen the spirit of religion and the spirit of freedom marching in opposite directions. But in America I found they were intimately united and that they reigned in common over the same country. Religion in America takes no direct part in the government of society, but it must be regarded as the first of their political institutions.

Raised an aristocrat, Tocqueville had every reason to be critical of American democracy. His family, considered elitists in France, had suffered at the hands of revolutionaries in search of democratic reforms. For that reason alone, Tocqueville had reason to despise democracy in any form. Yet his sense of fairness and objectivity would not allow him to bitterly dismiss the political process taking shape in America. Sensing that the ideals of his aristocratic upbringing were being rejected by the masses in France, he set out for America to learn of democracy's strengths and weaknesses. He wrote, "Religious nations are therefore naturally strong on the very point on which democratic nations are weak, which shows of what importance it is for men to preserve their religion as their conditions become more equal." Tocqueville understood the differences between the American and French revolutions. And the primary difference—a strong Judeo-Christian ethic—is what has led the two nations in distinctly different directions. The American Revolution initiated 200 years of democratic rule, without interruption. The French Revolution led to two centuries of instabilty, said the *L.A. Times*: "three revolutions, a directorate, a consulate, a restoration of the Bourbon monarchy, another monarchy, two empires and five republics."

FRANCE, 1989

Soviet leader Mikhail Gorbachev, speaking before the United Nations, said, "Two great revolutions, the French in 1789 and the Russian in 1917, have exerted a powerful influence on the very character of the historic process." His comparison of the two revolutions is more accurate than many Frenchmen would like to admit. Both revolutions were sadistically bloody and godless.

When three million spectators viewed France's bicentennial parade on July 14, 1989, some were unsure **what** they were celebrating, according to *Newsweek Magazine*. Some who **did** understand the reason for the festivity argued whether there should have been a celebration at all. They questioned the validity of commemorating a period of unnecessary terror and ruthlessness.

Schama said, "In some depressingly, unavoidable sense, violence was the revolution itself." Edmund Burke wrote at the outset of the revolution that France could have chosen a more peaceful path to democracy. Many of

France's citizens agree with Schama and Burke and therefore protested the bicentennial celebration. They accused the government of glorifying a stain on its history.

Today, the violent rampage of 1789 is symbolized at the site of the Bastille by indentations in the pavement showing where the prison once stood. Said one Frenchman to the Associated Press, "For us, it was a horrible genocide, a lasting source of national shame." Writer Philippe de Villiers charged that the bicentennial celebrations ignored the violence which took the lives of aristocrats and peasants alike—anyone who defended the church and the king.

De Villiers claimed that France's revolution was the justification used by Lenin and Stalin for their purges of the masses in Russia. Israeli lecturer J.L. Talmon suggested in 1952 that the French Revolution concept of a "general will" encouraged Marxist governments to deny individual freedoms for the "collective good."

The legacy of the French Revolution is not that of liberty; rather, it is more frequently remembered for the multitudes who were beheaded by guillotines. Miniature guillotines are sold by the thousands each year in France, mostly to tourists. In some respects this instrument of execution has become a symbol of the nation's heritage.

One woman, Manon Roland, who lived during the revolution, perhaps best summed up her nation's ill-conceived motives. At one time she had supported the revolution, but later rejected its violent chapters. Thus, she was sentenced to death. While having her head lowered beneath the guillotine, she said, "Liberty, O Liberty, what crimes are committed in thy name."

Americans, meanwhile, have tended to enshrine the French Revolution and place it on par with their own struggle for independence. To do so, is to either justify or ignore the heinous crimes lying in the wake of the French Revolution. Retired Chief Justice Warren Burger claimed erroneously that it was the hatred of tyranny which had inspired the revolutionaries in both countries. Burger said if the violence in France was more severe, it was because "the provocations that led to (France's) revolution were more severe than those that led to ours."

In July, 1989, government officials from both the United States and France gathered on the steps of the Jefferson Memorial to mark the anniversary of the storming of the Bastille. That day school children sang, bands played, and senators joined in reading the "Declaration of the Rights of Man."

The tie between the two nations has been long and cordial, and most would agree that France's philosophies have had a profound influence on the evolution of Western thought. To some degree, the secularistic ideologies exported by French thinkers have become foundational to the present consensus in America. French Ambassador Emmanuel de Margerie said that Voltaire, Rousseau, and other French thinkers had heavily influenced Thomas Jefferson's version of the Declaration of Independence. In other words, he was incorrectly suggesting that the two revolutions were based on the same secularistic ideology. American schools are also mistakenly touting the heroic nature of the French Revolution. One teacher, quoted in the *New York Times*, said, the French Revolution was "the big bang of revolutions. It made palpable the ideas of individual rights, national self-determination, and written constitutions."

Americans who embrace the French Revolution as a momentous occasion are either ignorant of history or they are espousers of Secular Humanism—the instigator and product of the regrettable upheaval.

THREE

POLITICAL ARENA: ONE NATION UNDER GOD?

It is the duty of nations, as well as of men, to own their dependence upon the overruling power of God and to recognize the sublime truth announced in the Holy Scriptures and proven by all history, that those nations only are blessed whose God is the Lord.

—Abraham Lincoln

The political marketplace has been a primary battle-ground for the spiritual allegiance of America. As in the days of the Scopes Trial, two forces are locked in a contest to determine whether America will return to her Judeo-Christian heritage or fully embrace secularistic ideals.

Government leaders are the pawn pieces in this chess match. Thus, secularists have lobbied endlessly to influence the perceptions of elected officials and campaigned tirelessly to elect candidates who will support liberal legislation. In more recent years, Christians have begun to understand that they must once again become a component of the political system if the representative government is to be truly representative. No longer can Christians assume that government will endeavor to protect religious rights or that it will fight to uphold a biblical ethic. The political arena is brimming with secularists seeking every opportunity to defame Christ and deny Christians their rights.

Throughout history, governments have either been an ally of religion or an antagonist; seldom neutral. Government's treatment of religion has often been determined by the degree to which our national leaders are committed to God, and therefore, the faith, or lack thereof, of our elected officials has had a direct bearing on the moral fiber of America. As in the Old Testament, when Israel's leaders were in apostasy, the people followed. To a certain extent, the same holds true today. A major portion of our population—perhaps subconsciously— will follow the spiritual tone or mood set by the president and other members of the political hierarchy.

One cannot disassociate the personal faith of elected officials from their governmental decisions. Their faith in God, or lack thereof, certainly influences how they vote, what they promote, and what image they project to society. At times they have contributed to the deliquency of the nation by the example set by their personal lifestyle. Other elected officials, since the founding of the nation, have made legislative attempts to secularize America. They have participated in decisions and propagated ideals which were contrary to God's Word. These same secularists have sought to use the political arena to revise the intent of the Constitution, maneuver the Supreme Court, and cripple the Church.

CONSTITUTIONAL DEBATE

When the final draft of the United States Constitution was ratified in 1787, as James Madison said, it was "a constitution for the ages"—a document which need not undergo revision with every societal mood swing or political fad.

A heated debate surrounded the ratification, however. It was to be a debate which would have a lasting effect on the secularization of America. Alexander Hamilton led the Federalist's contention that it was unnecessary to add a Bill of Rights to the Constitution, for, in the long run, he felt it would create problems of its own. Hamilton feared the Bill of Rights "would contain various exceptions to powers not granted [the federal government]; and, on this very account, would afford a colorable pretext to claim more than was granted."

The anti-Federalists opposed the Constitution in its final form because they believed the Bill of Rights was necessary to secure man's freedoms. They convinced enough of their contemporaries that the Bill of Rights was later added to the Constitution in 1791. As Hamilton accurately predicted, however, it proved to be a source of contention, especially in recent years. The meaning of the First Amendment of the Bill of Rights, in particular, has proven to be hotly contested. The Amendment reads, "Congress shall make no law respecting the establishment of religion, or prohibiting the free exercise thereof, or abridging the freedom of speech or of the press; or the right of the people peaceably to assemble, and to petition the government for a redress of grievances."

In the last fifty years, judges, attorneys, and elected officials possessing an anti-church perspective have maintained the First Amendment prohibits government from having interaction with religion. To the contrary, others have declared that it prevents government from establishing a national religion or giving any one religious denomination preferential treatment over another—thus, it says, "Congress shall make no law respecting **an** establishment of religion" as opposed to "**the** establishment of religion." Herein lies the essence of the "separation of church and state" debate.

Joseph Story, a Harvard law professor and Supreme Court justice, was the leading constitutional scholar of the 1800s. He maintained the Amendment was written to free religion from state control:

> Probably at the time of the adoption of the Constitution, and of the amendment to it now under consideration, the general, if not the universal sentiment was, that Christianity ought to receive encouragement from the state, so far as was not incompatible with the private rights of conscience and the freedom of religious worship. An attempt to level all religions, and to make it a matter of state policy to hold all in utter indifference, would have created universal disapprobation, if not universal indignation.

Authur J. Stansbury's *Elementary Catechism on the Constitution of the United States* was published in 1828 and used extensively in public and private schools. It discussed the intent of the First Amendment as perceived by Americans during that period:

Question: What was the subject of the First Amendment?
Answer: the subject of religious freedom.

Question: What do you mean by that?
Answer: I mean the right every man has to worship God in such way as he thinks fit, without being called to account for his opinions, or punished for them.

Question: Is this a sacred right, which ought to be guarded with the greatest care?
Answer: Certainly. God alone is the Judge of our religious belief and service, and no man has a right to interfere with it, so long as it does not lead us to injure or disturb our neighbor. A great part of the misery and oppression which has existed in the world, began with forcing men to do what their conscience disapproved.

Question: What amendment was made in the Constitution on this subject?
Answer: Congress was forbidden to make any law respecting an establishment of religion; that is, giving preference to any one form of religion above another, and making laws to support it; or making laws to prevent men from freely holding or observing any particular form of religious belief and practice.

Darwininans within the government and judicial system, who taught the Constitution was meant to evolve as society evolved, began practicing in the late 1800s what some deemed was constitutional engineering. They began interpreting the Constitution according to their secular beliefs with little or no regard for the intentions of the framers. Thus, as Hamilton had feared, the First Amendment was reinterpreted and a wall of separation between the church and state was imposed on the Constitution.

Since then, a myriad of politicians, attorneys, and activists have engaged in a lasting argument concerning the meaning and intent of the First Amendment.

Robert Cord, author of *Separation of Church and State,* said:

The documented public actions of the Framers of the First Amendment, including James Madison, and those of our early Presidents and Congresses indicate that the constitutional doctrine of separation of church and state to them meant that no national religion was to be instituted by the Federal Government; nor was any religion, religious sect, or religious tradition to be placed in a legally preferred position. It is not surprising then that the non-discriminatory use by government of religious institutions—such as schools—to accomplish goals within the government's authority was not considered by the Founding Fathers a violation of the Constitution. No matter what the Supreme Court, and some prominent constitutional scholars have written to the contrary, the facts show that Washington, John Adams, Jefferson, Madison and their Congresses, all used, in one way or another, what they viewed as non-preferential sectarian means to reach secular governmental ends.[1]

THOMAS JEFFERSON'S WALL OF SEPARATION

No constitutional ruling or interpretation has done as much to cause the pendulum of spiritual awareness to swing away from God as the First Amendment "separation of church and state" fiasco. This issue embodies the secularization that has transpired over the last two centuries. The court's separation ruling has harnessed the Church to the delight of secularists. But not even Jefferson, who is credited with delineating the intent of the First Amendment, would have applauded the posture taken by the Supreme Court.

During his campaign for president, Jefferson had been criticized by a group of Baptist ministers from Danbury, Connecticut. They feared his presidency would result in an infringement on their religious liberties. Jefferson responded in a private letter:

> Believing that religion is a matter which lies solely between man and his God, and that he owes account to none other for his faith or worship, that the legislative powers of government reach actions only, and not opinions, I contemplate with sovereign reverence that act of the whole American people which declared that their legislature should 'make no law respecting an establishment of religion, or prohibiting the free exercise thereof, thus building a wall of separation between church and state.'

Critics of church-state relationships have pointed to Jefferson's "antagonism" of religion as a means of underscoring his motivation behind the wall of separation statement. Though he was not a self-professed follower of

Jesus Christ, neither was he the atheist secularists make him to be. Undoubtedly, while serving as foreign minister to France, Jefferson assimilated secular thought; but his decisions and writings clearly suggest, said biographer Dumas Malone, he regarded religion as a "wholly private" matter and that he understood the value of religion in American society.

Jefferson's 1803 treaty with the Kaskaskia Indians provided funding to build a church and support other religious needs. He also extended an act in 1804 which allowed land grants for the Society of United Brethren to assist the organization in evangelizing the Indians.

In 1808, Jefferson said:

> I consider the government of the United States as interdicted by the Constitution from meddling with religious institutions, their doctrines, discipline or exercises. This results not only from the provision that no law shall be made respecting the establishment, or free exercise, of religion, but from that also which reserves to the states the powers not delegated to the United States. Certainly no power to prescribe any religious exercise or to assume authority in religious discipline, has been delegated to the general government.

It would be improper to infer that Jefferson did not possess reservations about government pursuing an intimate relationship with religion, especially when it came to endorsing one particular denomination over another. Conceivably, this was his motive for campaigning to de-establish the Episcopal Church as **the** church of Virgina.

He also refused to issue a presidential proclaimation for a day of prayer. Jefferson said:

...it is only proposed that I should recommend, not prescribe a day of fasting and prayer. That is, that I should indirectly assume to the United States an authority over religious exercises, which the Consititution has directly precluded them from.... I do not believe it is for the interest of religion to invite the civil magistrate to direct its exercises, its discipline, or its doctrines.

Jeffersons's "wall of separation" statement did not effect legislation until 1947 with the *Everson v. Board of Education* case, also known as the *Parochial School Bus Transportation* case. Everson challenged a New Jersey practice of using tax monies to subsidize the transportation of students to parochial schools. He claimed the state was violating the First Amendment by giving preferential treatment to religion. The case went to the Supreme Court where Justice Black, writing for the majority, said:

The 'establishment of religion' clause of the First Amendment means at least this: Neither a state nor the Federal Government can set up a church. Neither can pass laws which aid one religion, aid all religions, or prefer one religion over another. Neither can force nor influence a person to go to or to remain away from church against his will or force him to profess a belief or disbelief in any religion. No person can be punished for entertaining or professing religious belief or disbelief, for church attendance or non-attendance. No tax in any amount, large or small, can be levied to support any religious activities or institutions, whatever they may be called, or whatever form they may adopt to teach or practice religion. Neither a state nor the Federal Government can, openly or secretly, participate in the affairs of any religious organizations or groups and vice versa. In the words of Jefferson, the clause against establishment of religion was intended to erect a 'wall of separation between church and state.'

Black's summary would be the start of an avalanche of cases against the church and a severing of ties between government and religion.

RELIGION AND ELECTIVE OFFICE

Fundamental religious beliefs were once a prerequisite to holding public office even though the framers made it clear in the Constitution that "no religious test shall ever be required as a qualification to any office or public trust under the United States." A religious test—a public confession of a candidate's faith in God—has, until recent years, been an important element of a campaign. The Christian consensus was so strong in early American society that a politician would have found it difficult to be nominated without stating his trust in God.

Although today our elected officials are not required to recite a religious oath to serve the people, the president of the United States is still required to state his dependence on God when taking his oath of office. He pledges to support the Constitution "with God's help."

By 1868, the following oath had become the standard for many elected officials: "I do solemnly swear that I will support and defend the Constitution of the United States against all enemies, foreign and domestic.... So help me God."

North Carolina, early in the state's history, had its

own Declaration of Rights. It contained a statement guaranteeing freedom of worship. The state constitution, however, said that anyone denying the existence of God or the Old or New Testaments was not capable of holding public office. This was indicative of the state's Christian consensus and the general public's determination to have elected officials who possessed a deep faith in God.

Through the years, many religious requirements for candidates were abolished. The last requirement of this kind was stricken from the lawbooks in 1961 in *Torcaso v. Watkins*. The courts held unconstitutional a Maryland law requiring an elected official to hold a belief in God.

ABRAHAM LINCOLN AND THE BIBLE

If indeed Jefferson served to diminish religion's influence in the political arena, Abraham Lincoln, most assuredly, made the Bible the cornerstone of his presidency.

Two years after ascending the steps of the White House as this nation's sixteenth president, Lincoln called for a national day of prayer: "It is the duty of nations as well as of me to own their dependence upon the overruling power of God...and to recognize the sublime truth, announced in the Holy Scriptures and proven by all history, that those nations only are blessed whose God is the Lord."

Lincoln had read the Bible his entire life and relied upon it during turbulent times. So when he stepped to the podium to give his second inaugural address, he reminded the nation of God's role in the affairs of men:

> The Almighty has His own purposes. 'Woe unto the world because of offences for it must needs be that offences come; but woe to that man by whom

the offence cometh.' If we shall suppose that American slavery is one of those offences which, in the providence of God, must needs come, but which, having continued through His appointed time, He now wills to remove, and that He gives to both North and South, this terrible war, as the woe due to those by whom the offence came, shall we discern therein any departure from those divine attributes which the believers in a Living God always ascribe to Him? Fondly do we hope—fervently do we pray—that this mighty scourge of war may speedily pass away. Yet if God wills that it continue, until all the wealth piled by the bond-man's two hundred and fifty years of unrequited toil shall be sunk, and every drop of blood drawn with the lash, shall be paid by another drawn with the sword, as was said three thousand years ago, so still it must be said 'the judgements of the Lord, are true and righteous altogether.'

Lincoln's influence on the level of spiritual awareness in America can be traced to his willingness to publicly profess his faith in God. During one campaign he said, "I have never denied the truth of the Scripture" and "I do not think I could myself, be brought to support a man for office whom I knew to be an open enemy of, and scoffer at, religion."

A PRESIDENT AND HIS BOTTLE?

When word reached the United States capitol that more than thirteen thousand Union soldiers had been killed, wounded, or were missing from the battlefield, officials were distraught. Their emotions turned to rage, however, when rumors hit Washington, D.C., that General Ulysses S. Grant was drunk during the battle. Some called for President Lincoln to dismiss the general for intolerant behavior. But Lincoln, instead, chose to endure the wave of criticism. He claimed Grant was indispensable to the war efforts. "I can't spare this man," he said. "He fights."

Grant's reputation for behavior unbecoming to an officer followed him throughout his military life and into the White House. Stories of his drunken sprees and tales of his ineptitude have persisted through the years. Stephen B. Oates, author of *With Malice Toward None*, said, "Grant may have had his troubles with the bottle earlier in his life, but by the Civil War he seems to have imbibed no more than most army officers in that hard-drinking time. He enjoyed his glass, and on rare occasions may have enjoyed one too many, but there is no documentary evidence that he was the chronic drunk his foes made him out to be."

The public's perception of Grant, though possibly inaccurate, was that of a non-religious, frolicking man with, nonetheless, exceptional leadership qualities. Thus, in spite of his suspicious reputation, he was elected president of the United States—largely for his heroic efforts to defeat the Confederate's General Robert E. Lee.

Grant's presidency was beset with controversy. Members of his cabinet and staff were allegedly filling their pockets with gifts from big-business in exchange for governmental favors. Grant himself came under attack when his brother-in-law, Abel Corbin, became involved in a scheme to corner the supply on gold. Corbin, who was hired by financiers Jay Gould and Jim Fisk, tried to persuade Grant to keep the government from selling gold. The public assumed Grant was consorting with business tycoons as well, which further tarnished his image.

Though Grant was a hero to many, he nor his presidency did much to nurture a religious consensus in the country. If anything, the nation was left searching for an identity. But this was an era when the public's perception of the president dealt a more severe blow to the nation's attitude toward religion than any single policy decision he made.

In 1876, during the last year of Grant's administration, he sent a farewell message to Congress. He said he had entered office with limited political experience and thus had made mistakes. He then apologized, wishing he had done a better job. Biographer Gene Smith said, "His presidency was accounted to have been the most lamentable in history, and the judgement was continued and confirmed by later generations."

TEDDY ROOSEVELT'S STICK

"Walk softly and carry a big stick" became President Teddy Roosevelt's motto after becoming president in 1901. His slogan reflected a new identity, a new attitude of a burgeoning nation—an attitude of self-sufficiency, pride, and prominence. Roosevelt embodied this groundswell of American patriotism which actually nipped at the heels of self-exaltation.

Teddy Roosevelt came to Washington, D.C., as the vice president of William McKinley after a prominent career as a member of the Rough Riders and governor of New York. He became president when McKinley was assassinated. Politicians, publishers, and business tycoons watched with discerning eyes as this "cowboy" took charge.

Roosevelt's presence was felt immediately. He wielded influence over the military like he had over a bridled horse. He was not hesitant to use the armed forces in conflicts around the world if he thought it was in the best interest of the United States. *The Seven Worlds of Theodore Roosevelt* author, Edward Wagenknecht, wrote, "Now, Roosevelt had always maintained that a state which cannot enforce its rights cannot expect to receive them in this world." During his seven years in office, troops were exported to foreign lands and critics, according to the *American Educator Encyclopedia*, accused the president of "recklessly violating his constitutional limitations, of invading the rights of Congress, and of being dangerously warlike."

It was this boldness, arrogance, and leadership which won Roosevelt re-election in 1904 by an overwhelming margin. He had flexed the muscle of the United States abroad, given the nation a sense of self-sufficiency, and nurtured the belief that fighting was sometimes necessary to protect self-interest.

While his predecessors' words often advocated a dependency on God for the country's protection and provision, Roosevelt chose to center his public addresses on American fortitude, might, and worldwide influence.

PROGRESSIVISM AND THE PROHIBITION MOVEMENT

Roosevelt entered office at a time when government was often bending to the whims of capitalistic kingpins. Prior to his election, companies had expanded and built monopolies without constraint; legislation was being written to appease the warlords of big business— the men who, with one word, could determine the fate of a politician. The Progressive movement, which was strongly advanced by the Christian community, helped bring an end to this economic domination.

James H. Timberlake's book, *Prohibition and the Progressive Movement*, summarized the period between 1900-1920:

> The Progressive Movement of these years came as a reaction to a long period of dominant conservatism during which the nation had undergone a rapid transformation from a predominantly rural to an urban-industrial society....The Progressive Movement endeavored to come to grips with the two great problems threatening American democracy: the growing power of big business on the one hand, and, on the other, the mounting discontent of the lower classes, especially among urban-industrial workers. It sought to solve these two problems by democratizing the machinery of government and using government to control big business and to improve the lot of the underprivileged.[2]

As government began to assume the role of caretaker, there emerged a subtle shift in public dependence on God and church to a subconscious reliance on government to provide and protect the common man.

There were some, however, who sensed the public shifting its allegiance from God. This change, it should be noted, was more non-verbal than verbal. But a symptom of this shifting consensus resulted in something tangible—an increasing rate of alcoholism. Chuck Colson reported, "Not until 1970 did per capita consumption of alcohol again reach pre-Prohibition levels."

December 18, 1917, Congress adopted the Eighteenth Amendment to the Constitution, prohibiting the manufacture, sale, and transportation of alcoholic beverages. It went into effect in 1920. In *The Culture of the Twenties*, editor Loren Baritz said, "Defenders of Prohibition were seeking ways to preserve what they believed to be traditional American values against the corrosion of time; they argued that Prohibition was necessary for the moral strength of the nation...and to protect families of drunkards."

Most Protestant churches came to support total abstinence rather than moderation, for alcohol was viewed as a vice which kept men and women from finding God. This sentiment was fueled by large evangelistic crusades and fervent preachers who described alcohol as "the devil's elixir"—a potion that would lead to a decline of morality in America.

Prohibition was envoked because those in small towns "exercised their power over the nation through their values, attitudes and ideals.... This noble experiment was preeminently the creature of the provincial, middle class, Protestant, white American," said Baritz. (Of the 197 House representatives who supported the Amendment, 129 were from towns less than ten thousand.)

George Mowry, editor of *The Twenties*, added:

> The conflict was in some degree waged between an older North European American stock devoted to the Protestant ethic, with its emphasis upon individualism, hard work, sobriety...and the newer immigrant folk crowding the cities, by origin from Southern and Eastern Europe, by religion Catholic and Jewish, and by tempera-

ment devoted to more personal indulgence and paternalistic ways of thought inspired by either political or religious consideration.[3]

While many turned to government to protect their interests, said Timberlake, Christians had other plans:

> ...evangelical Protestantism sought to overcome the corruption of the world in a dynamic manner, not only by converting men to belief in Christ but also by Christianizing the social order through the power and force of law. According to this view, the Christian's duty was to use the secular power of the state to transform culture so that the community of the faithful might be kept pure and the work of saving the unregenerate might be made easier. Thus the function of law was not simply to restrain evil but to educate and uplift. Imbued with this idea of religion and law, evangelical Protestantism naturally turned to prohibitory legislation as a means of promoting its ideal of a sober society.[4]

To underscore the Church's stance against alcohol, many congregations changed from using wine to grape juice for the sacrament of the Lord's Supper. Although the vast majority of churches were solidly supportive of prohibition, there were several denominations that actively opposed it.

Churchgoers were not the only Americans campaigning against the sale of liquor. Many unchurched citizens recognized that the liquor industry had a secure grip on the purses of politicians who were in turn implementing pro-alcohol legislation. The industry was making a mockery of representative government.

One of the most outspoken and strongest organizations fighting alcohol consumption was the Women's Christian Temperance Union. The Anti-Saloon League was also influential in gaining public support for prohibition. The league was closely identified with rural America and with the Protestant clergy in small-town and country churches. "It called itself 'the church in action against the saloon....' People throughout America contributed to it as regularly as they did to their own churches.... No doubt many of these people felt that they were contributing to a religious war," wrote James P. Barry in his book *The Noble Experiment*. Many rural churches supported the organization because they considered themselves the protectors of "traditional American values against the immoral cities that were full of recently arrived immigrants."

Intemperence author Larry Engelmann said:

Despite vociferous insistence by the critics of prohibition that anyone who opened his eyes could see quite clearly that there was a good deal more drinking in America under Prohibition than there had been before, careful analysis does not support their contention. In fact, under prohibition there was a substantial decrease in the per capita quantity of alcohol consumed in the United States.... Prohibition, ironically, may have obtained some of its greatest successes in the very locations from which it got its worst press—on the college and university campuses.[5]

Prohibition put the church at odds with a host of politicians. It also was an attempt to use the political system to turn back a tide of liberalism and sin in American society. The Eighteenth Amendment was a concerted attempt by Christians and non-Christians alike to legislate morality.

But liberals fought back. This, too, was a war between the two philosophies of this world: secularism and Christianity.

A SAVIOR COMES TO WASHINGTON

When Franklin Delano Roosevelt became the Democratic Party's presidential nominee in 1932, he announced from the podium, "I say to you that from this date on, the Eighteenth Amendment is doomed."

True to his word, Roosevelt cut the budgets of the prohibition enforcement agencies. He also asked Congress to permit the sale of beer with a low alcohol content. Soon prohibition was a memory.

Repealing prohibition paled in significance to the other challenges facing Roosevelt's administration. When he entered office seventeen million were unemployed, banks were closing, and people were panicking. Roosevelt responded by unveiling his New Deal, a series of social programs which would serve to stimulate a lagging economy. Some thought his plan was nothing more than socialism. Others, including members of the Supreme Court, considered his plan unconstitutional. A duel of sorts emerged with Roosevelt trying to unseat conservatives from the Court so his legislation would be passed. Eventually, and largely due to public support, the constitutionality of the New Deal was upheld.

Roosevelt was a master of the press conference. He had the ability to captivate reporters and gain the confidence of the American people. For that reason, he con-

ducted nearly one thousand presidential press conferences in twelve years. He skillfully used the media to
restore a confidence in government which had unmerci-
fully faded following the stock market crash of 1929. He
once told Orson Welles, "There are only two great actors
in America—you are the other one."

Some historians have claimed that the Depression
elected Roosevelt, that it was the nation's hope for a new
beginning which helped Roosevelt win out over incumbent Herbert Hoover. Roosevelt campaigned on the promise that government would provide for those in need,
even though many of his proposals were equivalent to
programs already tried during Hoover's term. Upon
entering office, Roosevelt fulfilled many of his promises.
Aid and assurances were offered to everyone: investors,
farmers, the unemployed, bankers, creditors, and unions.
More than ever the common man looked to Roosevelt and
government as the "great provider."

Roosevelt did not necessarily, premeditatedly, attempt to detract from Americans' faith in God. It was just
a natural phenomena to "worship" one's provider and
rescuer: presumably Roosevelt and the federal gover-
ment.

The depth of the president's faith in God has been
brought into question, especially after revelations of his
private life. Basil Rauch, in his book *The Roosevelt Reader*,
wrote, "Roosevelt's spiritual perceptions were rather
shallow; he lived by a facile optimism enriched by very
broad human sympathies."

Roosevelt's speeches often spoke of an affection and
understanding of the Almighty. To the National Conference of Catholic Charities, he said, "With every passing
year I become more confident that humanity is moving

forward to the practical application of the teachings of Christianity as they affect the individual lives of men and women."

On his radio address, December 24, 1941, he said:

We are confident in our devotion to country, in our love of freedom, in our inheritance of courage. But our strength, as the strength of all men everywhere, is of greater avail as God upholds us. Therefore, I...do hereby appoint the first day of the year 1942 as a day of prayer, of asking forgiveness for our shortcomings of the past, of consecration to the tasks of the present, of asking God's help in days to come. We need His guidance that this people may be humble in spirit, but strong in conviction of the right; steadfast to endure sacrifice, and brave to achieve a victory of liberty and peace.

One must ask: was this political double talk at its finest, or, did Roosevelt have a deeper understanding of spiritual matters than his contemporaries gave him credit for?

JOE MCCARTHY: THE RUSSIANS ARE COMING!

In a letter to Pope Pius XII in 1941, Franklin Roosevelt said:

In so far as I am informed, churches in Russia are open. I believe there is a real possibility that Russia may as a result of the present conflict recognize freedom of religion in Russia, although, of course, without recognition of any official intervention on the part of any church in education or political matters within Russia.... There are in the United States many people in all churches who have the feeling that Russia is governed completely by a communistic form of society.... In my opinion...Russia is governed by a dictatorship.... I believe that the survival of Russia is less dangerous to religion, to the church as such, and to humanity in general than would be the survival of the German form of dictatorship.

Roosevelt had no way of knowing when he wrote the letter that American sentiment toward Communist Russia would take on a tone of paranoia. In 1950, a senator from Wisconsin, Joseph McCarthy, would make his first charge that 205 known Communists had infiltrated the United States government. Soon, forces rallied behind McCarthy's effort to expose them. What resulted was what some have dubbed a "witch hunt."

In July, 1952, McCarthy received a standing ovation at the Republican Convention. Two months later he went on national television to make additional accusations against leaders in the government. McCarthy would make similar claims in the months following, charging members of the television-movie industry and news media.

In the midst of this frenzy, organized religion vigorously opposed McCarthy. Then, in 1954, President Dwight D. Eisenhower divorced himself from McCarthy's campaign. That signified the beginning of the end of McCarthy's political career. Later that year, the Senate censured him for making unsubstantiated accusations.

The effect of McCarthy's crusade on the secularization of American society is certainly not monumental; however, the pendulum has now swung from the fear of communism of the 1950s and 1960s to a position which finds the philosophical differences between democracy and anti-God communism blurring. Naturally, Westerners are hopeful that there has been a change of ideology within the Soviet Union. They want to believe Soviet President Gorbachev is sincere and that his nation's goals no longer include world domination. This optimism, however, has led to a new found tolerance of communism, its ideology, and its leaders by United States citizens.

Dr. Francis Nigel Lee has accurately stated that Gorbachev has yet to renounce communism's goal of global indoctrination. Nor, according to Lee, has the leader denied communism's doctrinal, moral, and social errors: that there is no God; that "work... is to be performed gratis for the benefit of society"; private property and money are evils; the family is non-essential; education is to be "independent of parental control"; and all capitalistic societies are to be overthrown.

Still, the stigma of paranoia associated with McCarthyism has caused some Americans to label any skepticism of the intentions of Communist Russia as a rebirth of McCarthyism. Those who perceive Mikhail Gorbachev's *Glasnost* and *Perestroika* as a ploy to gain world acceptance and rescue a slumping economy have been pegged as paranoids. Individuals—particularly politicians—have become more fearful of the "McCarthyism" label than they are communism.

Some elected officials are more concerned with public opinion, avoiding negative labels, and getting re-elected than they are doing what is in the best interest of the American people. Secular lobbyists have exploited this weakness to shrewdly acquire the votes of self-concerned politicians.

THE PRESIDENT WE NEVER KNEW

John F. Kennedy will long be remembered as the epitome of the American dream: a good-looking, rich, well-educated war hero who grows up to marry a beautiful woman and becomes president of the United States. Those mental images fight to unseat the unforgettable footage of his assassination in Dallas, Texas in 1963.

Kennedy will be remembered for the Cuban missile crisis and the Bay of Pigs fiasco, his civil rights efforts, and his ability to capture the imagination of reporters and the American people at his press conferences. But the president's behind-the-scenes life has finally entered public view, and the stories have left their scars on a nation that wanted to believe in his greatness.

Washington news reporter Hedley Donovan said, "In private life, notwithstanding the storybook marriage, he soon resumed the diversions of bachelor days. Washington journalists gossiped knowingly, but few hints of his womanizing got into print.... After Kennedy entered the White House, the flagrant vulgarity and political recklessness of his philandering perhaps gave it an extra fillip."

Facts of Kennedy's covert bugging operation in the White House—taping conversations with staff people and other Washington insiders—raised eyebrows when disclosed years after his death. His alleged liaisons with Marilyn Monroe were also shocking, but perhaps no accusation has disturbed the public any more than Judith Campbell Exner's claim that former President Kennedy used her as a conduit to the mob. She claimed she set up private meetings with Kennedy and a Chicago crime boss and passed envelopes between the two men. The validity of her testimony has been brought into question, but, nonetheless, stories of this nature tend to undermine the public's trust of elected officials. The revelation of the "other" John F. Kennedy has caused many Americans disappointment. Their political hero has been reduced to a scoundrel and, surely, some have seen their faith in government officials fade as a result. And school children who were taught the exploits of the nation's youngest president now have in their possession unsavory chapters of his life.

Kennedy came from a devoutly Catholic family; he openly professed Catholicism. Yet, his private life appears to have been bathed in deceit. Said Donovan, "The flaws in the Kennedy character, and the rather meager accomplishments of his Presidency, do not seem to have shaken his powerful hold on the American imagination. Public opinion polls over the twenty years since his death have consistently placed him among our greatest Presidents."

One has to wonder if morality is still a prerequisite for public acceptance. Or, have we become so secularized that charm is more important than character? If more recent events are any indication, the flap over the alleged relationship between presidential candidate Gary Hart and model Donna Rice suggests Americans still desire leaders who at least appear forthright and wholesome.

The public image of a politician, however, is often more important to the electorate than the candidate's assortment of character flaws which may lie behind closed doors. Kennedy believed he was accountable only for his public life, and thus went to great lengths to steer public perception away from his personal activities.

RISE AND FALL OF RICHARD NIXON

When Richard Nixon took up residence in the Oval Office in January, 1969, some pundits dubbed him the most experienced man to ever sit in the president's chair. His resume included service as a United States senator and eight years as vice president under Dwight Eisenhower. His political career experienced a monumental setback when Kennedy outdistanced him in the 1960 presidential election; but he would survive. In the 1968 election, Nixon nosed out Hubert Humphrey. He and Secretary of State Henry Kissinger would later be lauded for their foreign policy, especially for their accomplishments in opening the door to China. Nevertheless, his terms in office would be marred by campus unrest, the Vietnam War, and finally the Watergate break-in and subsequent coverup.

In Jonathan Schell's book *Observing the Nixon Years*, he wrote:

> The history of the Watergate investigation is not a story of mounting public pressure, but, rather, is a story of successful efforts to consolidate widespread public suspicion of wrongdoing, which the powers of society felt free to ignore, into hard legal evidence, which no one—not the press, not Congress, not the courts, not the President, not even the public—felt free to ignore.

Nixon's fate was sealed when Judge John Sirica mandated the release of tape-recorded conversations from the Oval Office. Thus, save an eighteen-minute gap, the public obtained an unstilted glimpse of their president—an unveiling which defaced whatever gleaming image they had of their leader and, more distressingly, diminished respect for the office itself. Nixon was, in essence, defamed by his own unedited words.

When Nixon foresaw the end of his administration, he went on national television to announce his resignation. A few days later, the Nixons would be escorted to a helicopter where they would wave farewell to Washington, D.C.. It was the end of a celebrated political career. Nixon left office without much public sympathy, misunderstood, and humiliated.

The Watergate scandal left Americans with a disturbing impression of their leaders. They began questioning the motives of their elected officials; they became cynical of the public image of politicians as a whole.

Publicly, Nixon claimed to be religious and he encouraged the American people to pray, but, in the end, some critics dismissed his words as the rhetoric of a "political hypocrite." They challenged the validity of Nixon's so-called religious faith.

Chuck Colson, who served as a special assistant to Nixon, said:

> The President thirsted for a restoration of the old-fashioned values, something a restless nation could rely on and believe in. He once told me in the summer of 1970: 'If I do nothing else as President, I'm going to restore respect for the American flag.' And in the fall of 1971, after a long arduous session with his domestic advisers, ... Nixon confided a secret longing for something of 'enduring spiritual value.'[6]

Colson wrote, "... Nixon made the most startling statement of the day: 'You know, Chuck, I get on my knees every night and just pray to God.' I was stunned. For a man so proud he could never admit human weakness in any form... it was an amazing confession. From the tone of his voice I am convinced he was sincere."

Unfortunately, that was a side of the former president Americans may never come to know.

THE POLITICAL ILLUSION

Since Watergate, there has been a resurgence of public distrust for elected officials. This manifested itself on university campuses as journalism schools began, by the hundreds, manufacturing disciples of Bob Woodward and Carl Bernstein, the two *Washington Post* reporters who uncovered the Watergate scandal. Journalism graduates entered the workforce with a renewed determination to unmask deceitful politicians and unearth political crimes.

Simultaneously, the political illusion—that government could solve the problems of society—began to evaporate. The belief that government possessed a panacea for the ills of society is an illusion which had been fostered by Franklin D. Roosevelt, John F. Kennedy, Richard Nixon, and other presidents. Their campaign speeches rang with solutions and promises. The electorate often believed in them. Many citizens, up until Watergate, still believed government was the answer to all their concerns. But with the tragedy of Watergate, the nation began to reassess its confidence in government.

REPRESENTATION?

Americans, in recent years, have also begun examining the longterm effects of Congressmen using their influence to guarantee re-election. The June, 1989 issue of *Reader's Digest*, in an article entitled "Congressmen for Life: The Incumbency Scandal," said, "If you were a member of the House of Representatives, you would be more likely to die in office than be defeated for re-election." In 1988, 99 percent of the congressional incumbents were re-elected. The article pointed to three reasons why this is occurring: gerrymandering, which is the shaping of electoral districts to ensure the dominance of one party; political action committees, which are groups designed to take in large gifts for candidates; and "the congressional machine," which refers to the large staffs and budgets incumbents enjoy.

Once a Congressman is in office, even if he promotes secularistic principles, it is a tall task to remove him from office. This has led many citizens to a pessimistic view of their elected officials and system of government. They find it difficult to hold their representatives accountable for their voting record when re-election is virtually insured.

Because some representatives do not feel accountable to the people they are elected to serve, they use their votes to appease groups who can aid their next candidacy. Re-election often takes precedence over representing the people of his district or state. Though opinion polls may suggest the citizens of a given district favor one position, the representative frequently casts his vote in opposition, or vice versa. In Colonial America and up until the dawning of this century, the public expected their representative to represent the district's consensus on key issues. Today, "writing your Congressman" is considered by many as a futile exercise. Persons feel out of touch, as though their voice does not count. Despite the country's overwhelming opposition to child pornography, for example, it took Congress three years to get the Child Protection and Obscenity Enforcement Bill out of committee and voted upon. Some powerful bureaucrats—liberal politicians such as Edward Kennedy—slowed the process. They were wanting to eliminate adult obscenity provisions from the bill. Other politicians made attempts to delay legislation which banned the interstate transmission of obscene or indecent messages over phone lines despite the majority's view that dial-a-porn is improper for children.

THE DARK SIDE OF POLITICIANS

The alleged homosexuality of Congressman Barney Frank prompted *Newsweek Magazine* to publish a Gallup Poll with the headline: "Gays in Washington, Voters Aren't as Alarmed as Politicians Think." About 42 percent of the people polled felt Barney Frank should be reelected if the "incident (his alleged liaison with a male-prostitute) has not interfered with his ability to perform his duties." Forty-five percent said they could not vote for a candidate who was a homosexual. Yet, 60 percent said being a homosexual should not keep a person from serving in Congress. Ironically, months before news of his scandal broke, Frank was critical of Attorney General Ed Meese because **he** had been careless in his associations.

But the underlying issue supercedes the Frank affair. The larger concern is the influence that liberal officials in Washington are having on public opinion and morality. Their lifestyles and voting records tend to shape societal values. Edward Kennedy, for example, has certainly endeavored to liberalize the mores of this nation. Yet, despite his scandalous past, the senator's power and popularity continue to blossom.

At 11:15 p.m., July 18, 1969, Kennedy and twenty-eight-year-old Mary Jo Kopechne left a cottage party on a remote section of Martha's Vineyard called Chappaquiddick. Ten hours later the Washington secretary was found drowned in the back seat of Kennedy's Oldsmobile. He had driven the car off Dike Bridge into a pond. It took the senator nearly 10 hours to notify police of the accident— long after he had returned to his hotel room. He claimed he made repeated attempts to rescue Kopechne but was unsuccessful. Exhaustion and shock are the explanations Kennedy gave for the delay in notifying the authorities.

Many have questioned Kennedy's version of the episode. An article appearing in *Ladies Home Journal* raised these questions: "Had Ted Kennedy been having an affair with the...blond? Could the Senator have saved her life...? Did he contribute to her death by failing to report the accident to police?"

The truth may never be known but Kennedy's path to the White House has been derailed by uncertainties surrounding his character. Nevertheless, these uncertainties have not hindered his re-election in Massachusetts, nor have they caused a majority of the people in his state to challenge his legislative judgement. To many, he is a faithful leader, a man they will follow even if he leads this nation into a cavern of secularism.

SUPREME COURT POLITICS

The Supreme Court has become a political arena; some have likened it to the smoke-filled back rooms of the early 1900s, where, in fact, many congressional bills and political careers were determined.

Today, more attention is given to Supreme Court nominations than to the election of a senator or governor. And more interest is being paid to the opinions of those nominated, as signified by the rejection of Robert Bork in 1987. *Los Angeles Times* writers David Lauter and Ronald J. Ostrow said of the Bork hearings, "It is a story of pro-Bork strategists out-thought, out-maneuvered and out spent from the start by their liberal opponents."

The Bork rejection had nothing to do with his intellect or capabilities; it had everything to do with politics. Liberals rejected Bork because of his conservative perspective.

Lauter and Ostrow reported "Senator Edward Kennedy issued a harsh statement opposing the nomination [of Bork]. It implied that putting Bork on the court could bring back the days of 'back alley abortions' for women and segregated lunch counters for blacks."

Their *Times* article recounted a series of strategy meetings within liberal camps to plan a character assassination which would, in the end, defeat Bork. Anti-Bork advertisements and speeches by politicians painted him as the reincarnation of Adolf Hitler. Their distortions stirred the emotions of an uninformed public, which promptly, ignorantly, voiced its disapproval of the man.

One can expect future court appointments to be greeted with similar hostilities and political overtones. With the Supreme Court rapidly becoming a political hotbed, and politicians gaining more influence over the Court, the principles our forefathers based the Constitution on are in serious jeopardy. Secularists will and have used the political scene—including the Supreme Court—to dictate the future of this nation with little regard for the sanctity of the Constitution.

FOUR

EDUCATION: A CLASSROOM WITHOUT GOD

Education, to communism, requires a completely secular school independent of parental control; education to Christianity, must be Bible based and in accordance with the wishes of the Christian parents.

—Nigel Lee

Throughout the ages, those with secular perspectives have understood the importance of gaining control of the nation's children. If they could dictate which philosophy gained prominence in classroom textbooks, and which ideals were disseminated by school teachers, they knew they could change the Judeo-Christian consensus in America. To an extent, they have succeeded. Students today are being taught relativism, Secular Humanism, and values contrary to the Word of God.

THE BIBLE AND OTHER TEXTBOOKS

Education in the American Colonies was based on Christianity. Although the Bible served as the primary source of reading for youngsters, *The New England Primer* was also commonly used. Its lessons emphasized Calvinistic theology—that all men were born with a sinful nature and therefore were in need of salvation.

Noah Webster's 1828 *American Dictionary of the English Language* contained "the greatest number of biblical definitions given in any secular volume. Webster considered 'education useless without the Bible.' The Christian religion is the most important and one of the first things in which all children, under a free government, ought to be instructed.'"

Webster, known as the "schoolmaster of the nation," wrote various spellers and books containing the history and geography of the United States. In an early version of a speller, he prepared a moral catechism: "God's Word, contained in the Bible, has furnished all necessary rules to direct our conduct."

He gave much of his life to establishing a Christian educational system. He recognized that the only effective defense against the influence of alien philosophies of government or education was to construct a permanent foundation based upon the Word of God.

In 1838, textbooks still held a Christian slant. William McGuffey's *Eclectic Fourth Reader* devoted much attention to traditional values and biblical precepts. The preface of his book said: "From no source has the author drawn more copiously, in his selections, than from the sacred Scriptures. For this, he certainly apprehends no censure. In a Christian community, that man is to be pitied, who at this day, can honestly object to imbuing the minds of youth with the language and spirit of the Word of God."

The biblical accounts of Job, Christ and the blind man, and the celestial Kingdom were among the topics discussed in McGuffey's Reader. *World Book Encyclopedia* reported that "More than 120 million Americans purchased copies of the McGuffey Reader. Almost all American school children learned to read from it. The Readers played an important part in forming the moral ideas and literary tastes of Americans in the 1800s."

HORACE MANN AND JOHN DEWEY

By 1870, only 4 percent of the original Christian material remained in the revised version of *McGuffey's Readers*. The person allegedly responsible for initiating the removal of God from school textbooks was Horace Mann.

A group of atheists and socialists founded the Friends of Education Organization in the 1800s. Their purpose was to transform the American educational system. They had three objectives, according to Tim LaHaye's book *Faith of our Founding Fathers*: to "make school attendance compulsory; establish government sponsored 'free' schools; and form teacher training schools that they would control in order to prepare teachers of the future." They hired Mann as their first secretary of the State Board of Education in Massachussets. Later, Mann was to become the first secretary of education for the United States government. A Unitarian, Mann publicly promoted teaching morality based on Scripture—as he put it, allowing the Bible..."to speak for itself." But, privately, Mann sought to socialize education, to take it away from the church, and orientate teachers with secular philosophies.

No individual has made a greater impression on the twentieth century educational system than John Dewey. He said, "I believe that the school is primarily a social institution." Indeed, Dewey perceived the classroom as a place to instill values—his values. In 1934, Dewey "launched a journal of ideology, *The Social Frontier*, that urged teachers to find ways to advance 'the welfare and interests of the great masses of the people who do the work for society....'"[1] Dewey held a deep interest in Marxism and often invited Marxists to write for his journal.

Dewey was also one of the signers of the *Humanist Manifesto I*, which denied the existence of God, eternal life, the value of prayer, and creation. When Dewey, the secular humanist, gained a position of prominence in the educational system, he used his influence to spread his ideals. Meanwhile, many Christians were oblivious to what was being done to their children.

Today, men like Dr. Paul Kurtz have taken the mantle from Dewey and Mann—educators who toted an agenda to secularize society. Kurtz is the editor-in-chief of *American Humanist Magazine* and also a signer of the *Humanist Manifesto II*. On university campuses and in seminars across the country, Kurtz and his cohorts continue to preach the tenets of the Manifestos: that man is at the center of his universe.

THE SCOPES TRIAL

On the seventh day of the Scopes Trial in 1925, Attorney Clarence Darrow called Prosecuting Attorney William Jennings Bryan to the witness stand. The two men waved their fists at one another during the course of the trial, the fate of John T. Scopes paling in importance to the personal duel taking place between Darrow and Bryan. On the witness stand, Bryan found himself defending the meaning of God's Word and God's rightful place in the classroom. Darrow's interrogation of Bryan was an attack on the Fundamentalist contention that the Bible was inerrant and should be taken literally concerning creation.

Bryan responded, "I want the world to know that this man (Darrow), who does not believe in God, is trying to use a court in Tennessee...to slur at it [God's Word]...."

Darrow, an agnostic more than an atheist, held Bryan responsible for what he deemed a "foolish, mischievous and wicked act." He said, "If today you can take a thing like evolution and make it a crime to teach it in the public schools, tomorrow you can make it a crime to teach it in the private schools. And the next year you can make it a crime to teach it in the church."

Bryan made it clear that the primary issue in question dealt with a parent's right to determine what his or her child should be taught, rather than the validity of creation or evolution. Bryan was successful in combatting many of Darrow's arguments, although secular historians have unfairly made the "Fundamentalist activist" appear to be a narrow-minded, unworthy adversary. With the culmination of his political career, Bryan had turned to valiantly promoting a variety of causes: prohibition, women's suffrage, and defeating the rise of secularism in the classroom.

David Anderson, who wrote Bryan's biography, said:

Without having read Darwin he understood evolution, and without having read James he understood pragmatism, and he rejected both because they threatened the only reality it was possibile for him to accept: a reality in which reason and morality, hand in hand, gave the people control over their future. The orderly, moral growth of individuals and institutions, guided by God, was the essence of his political and personal philosophy, and actions and doctines that threatened either or that denied the traditional absolutes of democracy and Christianity were abhorrent to him. Both evolution and pragmatism invited a chaos he could neither accept nor tolerate. He demanded and promised an orderly progress no longer acceptable or possible for the more skeptical age that began with industrialism and materialism.[2]

Bryan's closing statement in the Scopes Trial was never heard because the case was submitted to the jury without argument. The speech later found its way into print, however. Bryan said:

The world needs a Savior more than it ever did before, and there is only one 'Name under heaven given among men whereby we must be saved.' It is this Name that evolution degrades, for, carried to its logical conclusion, it robs Christ of the glory of a virgin birth, of the majesty of His deity and mission, and of the triumph of His resurrection. It also disputes the doctrine of the atonement.

The Scopes Trial—though Bryan was in ill health, aged, and perhaps unprepared for Darrow's personal attack—was vital to the future course of classroom curricula. Bryan knew other states were eaves-dropping on the case, anxious to hear the jury's decision.

Darrow was successful—despite Bryan's efforts—in raising questions concerning anti-evolution laws. As Darrow had hoped, however, Scopes was convicted and fined $100. The jury's decision made it possible for Darrow to enter an appeal with the Tennessee Supreme Court to consider the consititutionality of the law.

Before the appeal was heard, Bryan suffered great ridicule from the press, degenerated physically, and finally died.

The decision in Dayton, Tennessee was eventually overturned on a technicality that the judge had set the $100 fine rather than the jury. However, three justices of the court held the law was constitutional. A fourth justice maintained it was unconstitutional which gave the secularists the foothold they were hoping for. Soon, other states began overturning their anti-evolution laws.

In an article entitled "Unbuckling the Bible Belt," the writers discussed some of the repercussions of the Scopes Case:

> Beaten back in the Scopes trial in 1925... fundamentalists retreated to rural and small-town America—especially the southern Bible belt. While mainstream Protestantism became increasingly secular in outlook—and spiritually undemanding—fundamentalists withdrew into a rigidly patriarchal and puritanical subculture of their own.

CREATION, EVOLUTION, AND TEXTBOOKS

Decades after the Scopes Trial, the theory of evolution would be found alongside the creational account in our school textbooks. Today, creationism has been deleted from most texts and evolution has assumed the posture of fact.

In the *Los Angeles Times,* writer Jessica Reynolds Shaver said:

> It's very odd that the California Curriculum Commission has voted to recommend to the State Board of Education that evolution be taught as uncontested fact—just when more scientists than ever before are contesting it. By claiming that 'there is no scientific dispute that evolution has occurred and continues to occur, the members of the ... commission are showing remarkable ignorance.[3]

Shaver, in her article, cited numerous credible scientists who have denounced evolution's theories. She asked, "Are they (the commission members) determined to maintain the status quo regardless of the facts, determined to make evolution true by a show of hands? Or, more likely, are they afraid of the theories that may have to be seriously considered if evolution doesn't have center stage?"

The issues surrounding the Scopes Trial of 1925 are still alive. Across America, church groups have stepped up a campaign to require the teaching of creation in public school science classes. And like the Scopes Trial, these isolated campaigns have national implications. California, in particular, is important. The state is one of the largest textbook markets, and thus is influential in setting national standards for publishers.

Anti-God groups have pooled their resources and formed alliances to resist the efforts of creationists. They claim that creation should not be taught because it cannot be tested scientifically. The carnival atmosphere of the Scopes Trial is destined to be replayed in Sacramento and other state capitols as Christians endeavor to gain equal exposure for creationism in the textbooks.

THE UNIVERSITIES

Most early American colleges were Christian institutions. And in the first century of the colonial era all 126 colleges were founded by a religious group or denomination. Harvard, William and Mary, and Yale, for example, were founded to support established colonial churches.

By the mid-18th century, numerous other denominational colleges were built. The governing boards normally included ministers. Daniel Boorstin, in his book *The Americans*, wrote, "Until nearly the end of the eighteenth century, the typical American college consisted of a president (usually a cleric, sometimes the pastor of a neighboring church) and a few (seldom more than three) tutors who were themselves usually young men studying for the clergy."

As colleges became more liberal arts oriented, and the curricula changed, new professors were hired, many of whom had been schooled overseas. Tim LaHaye said, "Because there were so few educators in our country who held masters and doctoral degrees, we developed a false intellectual inferiority complex toward the end of the century and began to send our bright, young educators to Europe to get their advanced degrees.... These degreed teachers became the heads of colleges." Returning from overseas, they brought with them a new wave of secular ideas.

Said Boorstin:

> As colleges became more dispersed, developing their interdenominationalism and their links with their local communities, they also became less identified with any particular profession. During the 18th century a decreasing proportion of American college graduates entered the ministry. By the second half of the 17th century even Harvard was drawing many sons of artisans, tradesmen and farmers. By the end of the 18th century only about a quarter of the graduates of all American colleges were becoming clergymen.

EDUCATION AND THE COURTS

The Supreme Court has methodically removed God from the classroom and attempted to make it a "neutral" environment. In making it "godless," the courts have given credence and preferential treatment to anti-God sects, including the secular humanists. Even though the Supreme Court ruled that secular humanism is a religion, in *Torcaso* v. *Watkins*, its doctrines are found in textbooks and preached by instructors.

In 1962, in *Engel* v.*Vitale*, the Supreme Court held unconstitutional the state of New York's policy that students recite a standard prayer in the public schools. This decision has remained unchallenged even though a Gallup Poll found that 66 percent of Americans favored voluntary prayer in public schools.

The following year in *Abington School District* v.

Schempp, the Court determined that Bible reading and the recitation of the Lord's Prayer in public schools were unconstitutional.

By 1980, in *Stone* v. *Graham*, the court held that the Ten Commandments could not be posted on the walls of public school rooms. Then, in *Edwards* v. *Aguillard*, 1987, the Supreme Court said the "theory of creation" could not be taught in public schools.

A RAPE OF HISTORY

Paul Vitz, professor of Psychology at New York University, conducted an exhaustive study for the National Institute of Education (NIE) of elementary and high school textbooks. The NIE is now part of the Department of Education. His purpose was to discover whether public school textbooks are biased against Christianity. His conclusion: "religion, family values and certain political and economic positions have been systematically omitted from children's textbooks."

His findings included:

> [In] 670 stories from grades three and six readers not one reference to representative Protestant religious life was found; sixth-grade social studies texts neglected, often to the point of serious distortion, Jewish and Christian historical contributions; aggressive feminist themes were prominent in many of the texts; none of the social studies books dealing with modern American social life mentioned the words 'marriage,' 'wedding,' 'husband,' or 'wife.'

The study also found that texts did not depict children praying or attending church, and major religious observances receive insufficient treatment.

Thanksgiving 1988, students nationwide read a fact sheet about the holiday, published by Universal Press Syndicate. It read: "The Pilgrims held the [Thanksgiving] feast to celebrate their good harvest. It was not a religious occasion, but they probably said blessings."

According to a study of the activities of tax-free foundations in 1954, millions of dollars were devoted to changing the public's perception of history. The Reece Committee, established by Congress, was under the direction of Norman Dodd. He claimed members of the Carnegie Foundation had hired professionals to rewrite history textbooks to suit their secularistic ideals.

An editorial in *USA Today* said:

> Studies by church groups and such civil libertarian organizations as People for the American Way and Americans United for Separation of Church and State have found that schools are dropping out religion where it should be left in. History texts have left out that Dr. Martin Luther King, Jr. was a Baptist preacher. Civics courses have left out religion's role in such current debates as that on abortion.... Teaching about religion can help our children understand our society. Religions are part of our history, and history belongs in our schools.[4]

Even television writer-producer and secular humanist Norman Lear criticized the absence of religious teachings in the classroom. Addressing the American Academy of Religion, he said:

I...part with those who are so fastidious in maintaining the separation of church and state that they would purge any reference to God or religion from the public schools. Among secularists, the aversion toward discussing moral values—let alone religion—can reach absurd extremes.... For fear of offending militant atheists—or fearful of denominations fighting each other—many textbooks barely mentioned the role of religion in American history.... How well have we been teaching American history if we have not been discussing the influence of religion upon our nation's fathers...?

CLASSROOMS IN THE 1990s

The classroom has become a warzone. Gang warfare and drug abuse have ushered violence onto campuses. Teachers fear weapons and physical retaliation when, just three decades ago, they had to concern themselves with chewing gum and uncompleted homework.

But perhaps the greater battlezone is the mind of a young person. Educators are scurrying to find programs that will improve attendance, test scores, and graduation percentages. All the while, they are ignoring the primary cause of many of their problems: the de-Christianization of the classroom.

Former Secretary of Education Willliam Bennett listed the characteristics of great schools in a *Reader's Digest* article: "Leadership, great teaching, involved parents, and a focus on values and character." Values and character are obviously lacking; thus, Bennett wrote, "The time has never been more ripe for parents and public to reassert control over their schools."

The anger swelling among parents prompted some leaders, including President George Bush, to suggest implementing a voucher system, whereby parents could select which public or private school their children should attend. Bush favored the plan to "give parents back their voices and their proper determining roles in the makeup of children's education, and...give schools a chance to distinguish themselves from one another."

SEX EDUCATION

Eagle Forum founder Phyllis Schlafly has noted that California has more sex education than any other state, and perhaps that is why it has the most sex-related problems.

The feud over whether sex should be taught in the classroom has given way to a debate over the shape of the sex-education curriculum. Organizations, like Planned Parenthood, have attempted to mold a curriculum many have found to be immoral and void of values instruction. Some counties have curricula in place which openly discuss, and in some areas, advocate abortion, homo-sexuality, and masturbation. These programs have had "little or no effect on reducing sexual activity, increasing the use of birth control, or lowering teenage pregnancy rates," reported syndicated columnist Cal Thomas.

Child therapist Bruno Bettlehiem said:

> In my opinion, sex education is impossible in the classroom. Sex education is a continuous process and it begins the moment you are born. It's in how you are bathed, how you are diapered, how you are toilet-trained, in respect for the body, in the notion that bodily feelings are pleasant and that

bodily functions are not disgusting. You don't learn about sex from parental nudity or by showering together. That's nonsense. How you feel about sex comes from watching how your parents live together, how they enjoy each other's company, the respect they have for each other.[5]

Nonetheless, Planned Parenthood is proposing that schools institute a curriculum which would virtually feature full-disclosure of sexual practices and issues to children. Simultaneously, they are pushing for schools to implement school-based health clinics—a place where students would receive sexual counseling and from which contraceptives would be distributed without parental consent.

In the Los Angeles School District, "Project 10" created an uproar. The program was established to provide counseling support to students struggling with their homosexuality and to provide information to students intrigued by the gay lifestyle. Some students were referred to gay centers by school counselors, where teens can be "recruited" by practicing homosexuals.

Homosexuality has bequeathed to society the deadly AIDS disease. And now under the guise of informing students of the dangers and prevention of the disease, gay activists and their values are gaining access to our classrooms.

Adolescents in California were exposed to a survey which included the following questions: "With how many people have you had any kind of sexual intercourse in your life? When you have any kind of sexual intercourse, how often is a condom (rubber) used? Do you have the skills to use a condom during sexual intercourse?" The mere questioning of students on these subjects suggests a social acceptability of fornication. This is nothing less than the state attempting to assume a parental role of teaching sexual values to young people.

The "entertainment" industry is assisting in this education effort by parading "experts" in front of cameras who advocate a sexually-reckless lifestyle. Television personality Dr. Ruth Westheimer is widely known among young people. She is the hostess of a program aimed at spreading her "do anything as long as you use a contraceptive" philosophy to teenagers. *What's Up, Dr. Ruth?* is shown nationally, giving her an opportunity to have a major effect on the sexual attitudes and values of America's youth. Westheimer said, "You (parents) should keep your nose out of the teen-ager's sex life. The teen-ager has the right to have or not have sex, using personal judgement. I don't want [parents] to delve into the sex life of their adolescent. With education done at an early age, the child knows where the parent stands."

THE ASSAULT ON GOD CONTINUES

In Omaha, Nebraska, ten-year-old James Gierke carried his Bible with him to school only to be told he was breaking the law by silently reading it during his free time on campus. A lawsuit ensued and James Gierke won his case. This, however, is indicative of how some officials attempt to stretch the "separation of church and state" ruling to deafen the gospel; it is also representative of the type of "persecution" and religious dissuasion taking place on campuses.

In Minneapolis, Minnesota, Westside High School officials attempted to deny a Bible club access to school facilities. The case was heard by the federal court, which rejected the school's argument that all other clubs on campus were part of the school's curriculum. Thereafter, the Bible club was permitted to meet in a room on campus.

In 1985, the Supreme Court held that "atheist" students had the right to attend class without being embarrassed because classmates prayed or discussed God. A case in Alabama, *Smith* v. *Board of School Commissioners of Mobile County*, determined that the child who believes in God has the same right to attend class without his views being belittled in textbooks. In the U.S. Court of Appeals, however, the decision was overturned, thereby discriminating against the Christian child.

In 1989, in Southern California, parents and school officials of the Hacienda-La Puente Unified School District were embroiled in a duel surrouding a series of books, *Impressions*, used by grammar school children. Parents disapproved of material bent on ridiculing parental authority and propagating New Age principles, violence, and evolution. When the dust settled, the books were removed. Other school districts using *Impressions* refused to bow to pressure from parents and pro-family coalitions, however. Proponents of the book series argued it was a violation of a child's First Amendment rights to censor what he or she read.

FIVE

ENTERTAINMENT: A PASSION FOR DISTRACTION

Right now there is a whole and entire generation
that never knew anything that didn't come out of
this tube [television]. This tube is the gospel, the
ultimate revelation.... This tube is the most awe-
some...force in the whole godless world.
—Howard Beale
"Mad Prophet of the Airwaves"
Network, 1976

Sociologists have long contended that the forms of
entertainment in a society are indicative of the culture's
values. They also suggest that a society's heroes are
reflective of what it considers important.

As American culture has de-emphasized God, its
passion for crude and violent entertainment has increased

significantly and heroes have achieved god-like status. As America's values have evolved, so has her perception of entertainment and entertainers.

BURLESQUE AND VAUDEVILLE

The saloon of the wild west was the forerunner to the nightclubs and taverns of the modern era. They were the entertainment centers of towns isolated from the rest of the world. The saloon's hitching post was a welcomed sight for weary travelers. Inside the distinctive swinging doors were floor shows, gambling, brawls, and alcohol.

In the early 1900s nightclubs gained prominence. Though initially they offered many of the same pleasures saloons had, some of these "watering holes" began featuring burlesque shows. Comedic-striptease acts sprouted across the country, and just as quickly, citizens rose in opposition to this menace to morality. Newspapers, businessmen, political officials, and religious groups protested the burlesque houses. Police raids followed. Frequently, however, the burlesque owners were acquitted and returned to business as usual.

In New York City there was a drive to deny business licenses to the burlesque houses. In fact, the *New York Herald Tribune* inaccurately reported in 1932, "The year about to sign off will be remembered as the year when burlesque shows were forever stopped." That year did not mark the death of burlesque, but the religious-social forces **were** successful in imposing obscenity standards on the burlesque houses.

While burlesque was fighting for survival in some parts of the country, vaudeville—a show which included song and dance, burlesque humor, magic, animal acts, and acrobatics—was securing its place as one of the dominant amusements among urbanites. Author Albert McLean said in his book *American Vaudeville as Ritual*, "Vaudeville arose in an era of crisis to offer the American people a definitive rhythm, a series of gestures which put man back into the center of his world, a sense of the human community, and an effective emotional release."

Myths (such as materialism) that were propagated in vaudeville, said McLean, were "sought out and catered to, that offense be given to no one and satisfaction to the greatest number." The first attack against vaudeville was launched by rural Protestant clergy, "who resisted with considerable ferocity the inroads made upon it by urban materialism."

Vaudeville managers understood the profitable wisdom of policing their own shows in an attempt to maintain an image of wholesome, mainstream entertainment. Certain words such as "damn" and "hell" were forbidden and seedy material censored. McLean said:

> For the vaudeville audiences themselves, the appeal to purity and uplift was more a snobbish identification with upper middle-class taste than it was a matter of religious conviction.... By 1915, it made little difference to the vaudeville managers whether or not clergymen attended their shows, but they kept a weather eye open for the social worker, with policeman in tow, out to preserve the integrity of the American home.[1]

"HURRAY FOR HOLLYWOOD"

The director of movies like *King of Kings* and *The Ten Commandments*, Cecil B. DeMille, was a force in Hollywood. When others scoffed at making a movie of "Sunday school stories," he stood firm in his contention that they were of value to society. He realized that the "Law of God is the essential bedrock of human freedom."

The movie-maker went to great lengths to research the Scriptures and seek the counsel of ministers and priests to ensure the biblical accuracy of his films, to depict God and Jesus Christ in an appropriate manner. The script for *The Ten Commandments* was three years in the making. During the filming of the movie, the aging director suffered a heart attack. Later he wrote:

> I did not tell the doctors what I was also thinking, that if my motives in making the film were what I thought they were, I would be given the strength to finish it. I was 73 years old. That was a lifetime long enough for a man to have learned something about the ways and power of God; and long enough to make it not so very important if one's greatest effort turned out to be his last. But what I told the doctors was that I proposed to be on the set a little after nine o'clock the next morning and to go on with my work.

From the birth of film, the medium's power to influence public opinion has been recognized and highly sought after in Hollywood. In his book, *An Empire of Their Own*, Neal Gabler said fifty-three of the eighty-five persons engaged in the production of movies during the early days of the industry were Jews. They took great care to avoid alienating the Christian community—partly because it was good business, partly because they wanted to find acceptance. It paid off, for during the 1920s, as Americans flocked to movie theaters, these Hollywood moguls experienced unprecedented wealth and fame. In the late 1930s Hollywood was transformed into a political machine. Film became a weapon used by the United States government and anti-Nazi groups. Today, many contend that Hollywood is controlled by individuals dictating another political-ideological agenda: secularism. The film *The Last Temptation of Christ*, for example, is a far cry from the days when DeMille and other noteworthy directors sought the counsel of the church. Many modern day directors and film productions are in defiance to everything godly. They have a reckless disregard for people's beliefs and give no consideration to the the effect they will have on the nation's Judeo-Christian ethic. *The Last Temptation of Christ*, when contrasted with *The Ten Commandments*, is indicative of the secularization of Hollywood. Forty years ago, a blasphemous film on the life of Christ would never have been released. Today, under the guise of "art" and free-speech, such films are distributed, screened by thousands of young Americans, and enter millions of homes via cable television.

In 1915 the Supreme Court held that moving pictures were not protected under the First Amendment. That ruling stood until 1952. But through the years numerous films were banned and censored. In 1921 the National Association of the Motion Picture Industry (NAMPI) adopted a self-imposed code to stem the tide of censorship. The code's taboo subjects included nakedness, gambling, drunkenness, offenses to religion and religious figures, prolonged passionate love, and "salacious" titles. The failure of this and other codes led politicians to enter a long-standing debate surrounding governmental control of the movie industry.

In 1933, studios and producers agreed to follow a Motion Picture Code, which stated, according to *Citizen*

Magazine: "No film or episode may ridicule any religious faith; ministers of religion should not be portrayed as comic characters or as villains; religious ceremonies should be carefully and respectfully handled."

Citizen reported that the code wielded "considerable influence over the content of motion pictures until the mid-60s." That is when the film offices of several churches stopped approving scripts and issuing seals of approval. In their place, the Motion Picture Association of America instituted a woefully permissive rating system.

Since then, Hollywood films, according to "Prince of Sleaze" director-producer John Waters, have purposely become more violent and sexual in content. When asked if America is "less shockable" than it used to be, Waters responded, "Yeah, there are fewer taboos now because Hollywood's co-opted it all. Hollywood makes shocking movies now. So there's no taboos left to break. So once you've broken all the taboos, then you have to refine it to get laughter and a sense of humor."

TURN THE CHANNEL, PLEASE

About 98 percent of the homes in America have at least one television set; about 64 percent have a VCR and two televisions in their home. In 1970, only 35 percent had two television sets and VCRs were just being developed. This truly has become a television generation—a generation which finds Sunday evening the most attractive viewing time.

Recent television programming has been the antithesis of the wholesome shows of the past: "Leave it to Beaver," "Ozzie and Harriet," "Dennis the Menace," "Lassie," and others. These were programs that encouraged traditional family values. Today, even the updated versions of old shows reflect an anti-family perspective.

In the 1950s, in an effort to "deflect criticism" and "ward off regulatory intrusions," a Code of Good Practice was established by the National Association of Broadcasters. The self-imposed code had minimal effect on programming, thus the Federal Communciations Commission stepped in and assumed the lofty role of being television's watchdog. For nearly a decade, network executives were fearful of legal hassles with the FCC. But soon the networks began chipping away at the FCC's authority and guidelines, and the Commission was unable or unwilling to retaliate.

In 1972, CBS's hit show "Maude" dealt with the issue of abortion; the script conveyed the impression that killing an unborn was perfectly acceptable. In response, prolife groups rallied against CBS, but the FCC would not become involved, and, although some stations refused to show the reruns, secularists had won a major battle in their quest to employ television as a tool for propaganda.

"Soap" made "Laugh-In" and other controversial programs of the 1960s appear mild by comparison. The show satirizing daytime soap-operas incited the wrath of many Christians. "Soap" devoted scripts to such topics as "premarital sex, adultery, impotence, homosexuality, transvestism, transexualism, religion...etc.." In the four months preceding the premiering of the show, about 22,000 letters landed at ABC—mostly in protest. Some advertisers became concerned with the threat that religious groups would boycott their products. But the noise of protest eventually decrescendoed to a whisper and the show continued on schedule with moderate success.

Kathryn Montgomery said in her book *Target: Prime Time* that NBC came under fire in 1974 for the showing of

Born Innocent for its graphic portrayal of a young girl being raped in a reform school. The public outcry prompted Congress to "put pressure on the FCC, which in turn put pressure on the three networks."

Once again, with the FCC's urging, the networks took action to enact a self-regulatory code by establishing family viewing slots between 7 p.m. and 9 p.m. But this satisfied neither the networks nor the segment of the public concerned with violence and sensuality on tel-evsion. The impact of "family viewing hours" was short-lived.

During the Reagan Administration, the FCC lost much of its authority. Networks again sensed the freedom to stretch the limits of viewing decency. Advocacy groups, realizing the FCC's lack of authority over the networks, began sending lobbyists to Hollywood in the 1980s to influence programming subject matter.

"Trash television" evolved because of a "toothless" FCC and society's lust for violence, sensuality and sensa-tionalism. The "trash tabloids" have been around for years but were tolerated due to the obvious limitations of the print medium and the general assumption that most of the reporting is fictional. But with the birth of programs like "A Current Affair" and "Hard Copy"—that are simi-lar in format to "60 Minutes" and "20/20"—viewers con-fuse their sensationalized features with verifiable jour-nalism.

Talk shows such as "Geraldo" and "Morton Downey, Jr." are meant to incite verbal brawls. They're intended to shock, to entertain, but, for the most part, they simply give airtime to deviants, perverts, and other anti-God constituents. Because ratings are so critical to a show's survival, even credible programs—including those which are news-oriented—have resorted to this brand of sleaze and sensationalism.

Newsweek Magazine did a feature on the new wave of television, saying, "...the tabloid virus, previously confined to the fringes of syndication, is gradually infecting prime-time network programming. In the simplest terms, if you can't beat 'em, join 'em." University of Wisconsin social historian Stan Schultz said, "We're convinced that we can't impact public policy and we've lost control of our kids, so we abide by the law of the Roman circus: a little blood here, a little sex there, and most people will be happy."

Newsweek also ran an article entitled "Whatever Happened to the 'Content Police'?":

> ...everything up to and including sadomasochism seems to be OK. Why have standards relaxed so drastically? Historically, the government has left direct content regulation to the broadcasters themselves, while still maintaining broad licensing power. And the networks say, simply, that as society's mores have changed, they have changed as well. They insist they air what mainstream America will accept.

The truth is that networks have closed their Standards and Practices departments. Consequently, there is virtually no internal or governmental watchdog. In an article "Censorship Fear Grips Hollywood," the *L.A. Daily News* reported that some television producers fear the new leniency may change as networks "come under increased pressure from advertisers, moral crusaders and big business."

Threats of leaving the networks have been made by a

number of advertisers, including the Chrysler Corporation. Chairman Lee Iaccoca called on producers to censor their own shows or his corporation would spend its annual $250 million advertising budget elsewhere.

Complaints from wary advertisers have quite often centered around violence on television. Perhaps they are beginning to recognize the social impact of the programs they are sponsoring. A study conducted by Dr. Brandon Centerwell found "a link between prolonged television viewing and the increased incidence of murders in the United States." And in 1964, a study by the U.S. Senate Subcommittee on Juvenile Deliquency found: "...on the basis of expert testimony and impressive research evidence, that a relationship has been conclusively established between televised crime and violence and anti-social attitudes and behavior among juvenile viewers.... It is clear that television is a factor in molding the character, attitudes and behavior patterns of America's young people."

An editorial appearing in the *Contra Costa Times* said:

Legislation by Senator Paul Simon, D-Ill., would take a modest step in the right direction. It would allow television programmers—stations, cable operators and networks—to write voluntary guidelines limiting violence.... In so doing, broadcasters should pay close heed to studies showing the constant drumbeat of violence can brainwash children into acting out aggressions with fists and even guns. Researchers have found children exposed to television violence are more likely to get into fights, while they are less cooperative with teachers and other students. The networks vigorously oppose Simon's bill, saying Congress is flirting with censorship. Merely permitting the self-restraint that once prevailed in broadcasting hardly encroaches on the First Amendment.[2]

Politicians are beginning to recognize the need for television moral codes, primarily because viewers are chiding advertisers, and, advertisers are in turn communicating these complaints to politicians.

Reaction to Pepsi's commercial featuring Madonna was so fierce that the corporation pulled the plug on the ad at a cost of $10 million. Several advertisers yanked their ad from the television series "Married... With Children" when a Michigan mother wrote letters detailing her dissatisfaction with the program's content. "I find it very offensive," Terry Rakolta said. "It exploits women, it stereotypes poor people, it has gratuitous sex in it and very anti-family attitudes."

Christian Leaders for Responsible Television, the group founded by the Reverend Donald Wildmon, has been instrumental in organizing Christians to voice their programming concerns to advertisers who control the purse strings of the industry.

But this is not soley a religiously-based issue. Columnists and politicians alike—many of whom do not profess Christianity—are recogized the need for a change in television. The *Washington Post's* Tom Shales wrote:

Who owns the airwaves, and what is the social responsibility of those who use them to make money? By congressional mandate, the airwaves belong to the public, and broadcasters who use them have a duty to do more than generate profits for themselves. Television is an enormously influential component of our social environment.... Maybe it's naive to imagine after all these years that television can be an instrument to enlighten and ennoble us as a people, but even a casual observer can see it's gone way too far in the other direction. The instrument is out of whack, and needs a good swift kick.[3]

Opponents see Shales' reaction to programming as an attempt to justify censorship. But as Shales added, "If this is censorship, it would appear the republic will survive it."

Religion lost its presence on network television years earlier, causing a 1989 *T.V. Guide* article to say, "We need more religion on prime time." The author said, "Religion is rarely mentioned in current prime time dramas or sit-coms that supposedly reflect the way we live now. Yet religion and spirituality are increasingly a prime (if not yet prime time) factor in contemporary life."

The reason for the neglect is obvious. As one Los Angeles attorney said, "It would be hard right now to imagine a more atheistic community than the people who make primetime TV and feature movies. The result is that it's almost impossible to find a Hollywood product with real human characters who make a decision based on religion."

CARTOONS, COMIC BOOKS, AND TOYS

Saturday morning cartoons have been under fire from concerned parents for many years. Now their fears have spread into other areas.

Batman, once regarded as a clean-living comic book hero and television good-guy, was portrayed in the 1989 big screen adaptation as a schizophrenic. Opening night, children sat in more than two thousand theatres across the country to view the hero they had grown to love. They were exposed to something quite different—a violent, mentally disturbed man.

According to Focus on the Family's *Citizen Magazine*, this is symbolic of the graphic violence, sexual explicitness, occult themes, profanity, and obscenity in comic books today. The article, "Mean Comics," details examples of rapes, sexual fantasies, murder, and suicide within the pages of these magazines.

In 1954, a U.S. Senate Subcommittee on Juvenile Delinquency held hearings on the subject. A Comics Code Authority was established to regulate content. By the late 1960s, publishers began ignoring the code and delving into subjects inappropriate for children readers. And no one stopped them.

The dangers of toy guns and other make-believe weapons has been widely chronicled, but the creation of newer toys deserves discussion. Demonlike creatures—made of plastic and cotton stuffing—line the shelves of toy stores. In 1989 Matchbox Toys began distributing a Freddy Krueger doll from the *Nightmare on Elm Street* movies. Donald Wildmon's group responded immediately, urging people to boycott the company and all stores handling the product. Parents were disturbed by the doll because Freddy is a character who has blades for fingernails and murders his victims in their dreams. When the doll's string is pulled, it says, "Pleasant dreams," or "Watch out, Freddy's back."

HOLLYWOOD'S HEROES

Hollywood need not invent characters to lead our youth astray when the personal lives of some of its celebrities monopolize the news. Their decadent and valueless lifestyles—at least as they are portrayed in the media—create an illusion of the status quo. The glitter and glamor of their opulent indulgences are depicted each night, waved in the faces of young people like a brass ring well within their grasp.

James Dean, Elvis Presley, and others were once the idols of rebellious teenagers; but today a new heroine has emerged from Hollywood's elite to become a guru to a restless generation in search of happiness. Actress Shirley Maclaine has more than ten million copies of her New Age books in print and made-for-television movies about her life and religion have been shown in prime time.

In an interview with Waldenbooks, Maclaine was asked, "You've been credited with triggering America's interest in New Age. How do you feel about that responsibility?" She responded, "All I know is that I've been a seeker and a searcher all my life. All my traveling was about trying to find myself. And that's what New Age is—looking into yourself to discover who you are."

Thousands have been led astray by Maclaine's example and the empty philosophies promoted by celebrities before her. Throughout history, individuals have followed secularistic politicians, actors, musicians and athletes, never realizing that those they were following were "guides" still searching for the truth.

THE BIRTH OF ROCK 'N' ROLL

When Elvis Presley performed on "The Ed Sullivan Show" in 1955, no one foresaw the impact it would have on the music industry. Few realized the effect Presley would have on American culture. The Sullivan show gave Elvis and rock 'n' roll new stature in the music world and moderate acceptance in middle America. Though Presley had debuted on television before, it was Sullivan's promotion genius which made the rock singer front page news. To add mystery and precaution to the event, Sullivan ordered his cameramen to film the hip-swinging Elvis from the waist up. On subsequent shows, the camera gave the audience a full length view. Before long, young people everywhere would be mimicking and worshipping "The King."

Sullivan, in 1964, was the host to another group of budding rock stars—the Beatles. Jerry Bowles, in his chronicle of the Sullivan show, said, "To some (young people) the Beatles represented nothing more than a bit of relief from the despair [from the John F. Kennedy assassination] that had engulfed them. To others, more bitter, the Beatles represented the beginning of a rebellion. To them, the Beatles were to be the Fort Sumter of the War of the Sixties." Sullivan was delighted by the hysteria created by the Beatles' appearance, though realizing "he would be in for some grief for leading the youth of America astray."

One newspaper wrote:

> Britons and Americans have had their differences over Suez and Skybolt. There was even quite a to-do over the the Boston Tea party. But for sheer British ruthlessness, nothing can compare with the dispatch to the United States of four screaming, strumming young Liverpudlians with golliwog haircuts.

In the 1960s, young people began searching for spokespeople to voice and perhaps shape their philosophies. Musicians such as the Beatles' John Lennon accepted that responsibility. Youthful followers around the world read what he said:

> Christianity will go. It will vanish and shrink. I needn't argue about that. I'm right and I will be proved right. We're more popular than Jesus now. I don't know which will go first—rock 'n' roll or Christianity. Jesus was all right but his disciples were thick and ordinary. It's them twisting it that ruins it for me.[4]

Elvis, the Beatles, and other rock performers were emissaries in an era of shifting attitudes, from which came rock 'n' roll.

August 15, 1969 will live in infamy as **the** weekend of rock 'n' roll utopia. For three days in upstate New York the Woodstock Festival was held. Thirty-three musical acts played to an estimated crowd of 450,000 young people. Jimi Hendrix, Janice Joplin, The Who, The Grateful Dead, Creedence Clearwater Revival, Jefferson Airplane, and Joan Baez were among the performers.

It has been referred to as the "anti-establishment slumber party" and a "heathen hoedown." Woodstock, observers have noted, was a drug party rather than a social statement. It was rock 'n' roll heroes serving as demi-gods granting their permission on drug abuse and lasciviousness.

Although aspects of the hippy era have been assimilated into the mainstream of American culture, other byproducts of the '60s movement have reared their ugly heads—drug abuse, family breakups, sexual promiscuity, and AIDS. Music surely played a key role in rallying or inciting young people to participate in the cultural revolution.

Today music is still having an effect on the lifestyles of young people. MTV, which shows videos of heavy metal bands to new wave groups, is piped into nearly fifty million homes across the United States. The videos depict much of what Woodstock's performers professed—"do it if it feels good." MTV's rock videos are inundated with sex and violence. And by the hour, kids and young adults watch their heroes preach through music.

Newsweek reported, "MTV, unlike the passing fancy that was Woodstock, is solid, secure and here to stay. Its effect on the entertainment business has already been profound: TV shows from network drama to local news move differently because of rock video's quick-cutting visual style."

Heavy metal band concerts have also acquired stature around the world, groups often performing to screaming thousands. Lyrics are no longer suggestive; they are blatantly vulgar. Stage choreography has exceeded wiggling hips and dancing. Some "musicians" even tease the listeners with sexual movements and flashes of nudity on stage. Legislative attempts to require rating labels on albums and to impose an age limit to attend the concerts of certain performers have been met with cries of censorship from the music industry. In the name of protecting their profits, recording companies, agents, and artists are leaning on the First Amendment. Author Tipper Gore, wife of U.S. Senator Al Gore, told *Time Magazine*: the record companies are "strip miners, profiting from the sex and violence and ignoring the scars."

Former rock musician Robert DeMoss has alerted parents to the dangers of today's music. "Few parents take the time to sit down and help their kids steer through those voices out there in the world," he said. "The world is dumping all this garbage into the minds of kids without anybody helping them categorize what's right, what's wrong or what's pleasing to God."

PORNOGRAPHY EXPLOSION

Though some rock videos and rock concerts could be considered pornographic, a deluge of hardcore obscenity has spread like a bubonic plague across the land. Newsracks with obscene tabloids and x-rated cable television programming are at the disposal of the nation's youth. Child pornography and pornography depicting heinous crimes against women is being consumed at an alarming rate.

Secularists claim that consuming pornographic material is their right under the First Amendment. For fear of censorship, they pretend there is no correlation between pornography and sex-related crimes. They ignore a host of scientific studies and the testimonies of convicted serial killers like Arthur Bishop and Ted Bundy.

Bishop said, "Pornography wasn't the only negative influence in my life, but its effect on me was devastating. I lost all sense of decency and respect for humanity and life, and I would do anything or take any risk to fulfill my deviant desires."

In January, 1989, just before being executed in the electric chair, Bundy invited Focus on the Family's Dr. James Dobson to interview him concerning the part pornography had played in his crimes. Dobson later wrote:

> ...why did Bundy choose to convey that message through me? Because he knew the press would not permit his views to reach the people. There is no subject that agitates news reporters and talk

show hosts more than the link between sexual violence in the media and violence against women and children. Billions of dollars are generated on television and in print by the depiction and exploitation of violence. That colossal source of revenue is protected with vengeance by those who profit most from it.[5]

Bundy told Dobson that pornography fueled his fantasies and led to an addiction to obscene materials. He said pornography was "an indispensable link in the chain of behavior which led to the murders."

Afterwards, Dobson took a beating in the press, editorials charging him with exploitation and being an accomplice to Bundy's "showmanship." In response, Dobson wrote in his monthly newsletter, "I saw how they would use my participation to discredit the link between violence in pornography and violence against women." Dobson served on the Attorney General's Commission on Pornography. That commission found that "exposure to sexually violent materials has indicated an increase in the likelihood of aggression."

There is strong evidence that pornography can lead to serious sexual crimes. Numerous serial killers have linked their crimes with the use of pornography. The FBI interviewed thirty-six mass murderers and found that twenty-nine of them had used pornography heavily. The number of rapes in this country has also increased by more than 500 percent since 1960. Another study found that 86 percent of rapists regularly used obscene materials. About 57 percent of the rapists admitted to actually imitating pornographic scenes in their crimes. In Michigan, the police reviewed forty-eight thousand sex crimes in their state over a twenty-year period. They discovered that in

42 percent of the cases, "pornography was used prior or during the sexual assault."

The Catholic church has taken a strong stand against pornography. From the Church's Origins Documentary Service came a report entitled "Pornography and Violence in the Media: A Pastoral Perspective." It suggested the following as a major cause of the problem:

> Freedom of expression is said by some to require the toleration of pornography, even at the cost of the moral welfare of the young and of the right of all members of society to privacy and to an atmosphere of public decency. Some even falsely say that the best way to combat pornography is to legalize it. Faulty libertarian arguments are sometimes espoused by small groups who do not represent the moral values of the majority and who fail to recognize that every right carries with it a corresponding responsibility. The right to freedom of expression does not exist in a vacuum. Public responsibility for promoting the welfare of the young, for fostering respect for women, and for the protection of privacy and public decency indicates that liberty cannot be equated with license.

The courts and legislatures have not been too successful in repelling the onslaught of indecent materials. In a 1989 case involving porno-queen Traci Lords, the courts impotency was again revealed. A distributor of x-rated films was charged with racketeering and distributing obscene material. The *L.A. Daily News* reported:

> The judge ruled that although he personally found

the sexually explicit, violent tapes distasteful, he did not have the expertise to decide whether they violated the standards of a community as large and diverse as Southern California. The prosecution chose not to present expert testimony of the local standards of decency because of prior court rulings that said such testimony is unnecessary. [In 1973 the Supreme Court said experts were not necessary to prove obscenity.] Simply stated, hard core pornography... can and does speak for itself.

Though the Miller Standard in California allows each community to determine what is obscene, this case points out the importance of Christians voicing their objections to pornography—so judges will uphold the Judeo-Christian ethic. One community action group spoke so loudly the city forced pornographic newsrack owners to install blinders. Furthermore, citizens urged the city to enforce the penal code disallowing obscene matter to be sold in vending machines located on public sidewalks.

WHAT CONSTITUTES ART?

The artist called his creation "Piss Christ." Andres Serrano's photograph showed a crucifix immersed in urine. The photograph was to be displayed as part of a major exhibit in Washington, D.C., but the show was cancelled due to public outrage and a squabble over funding. The gallery sponsoring the exhibit had received $300,000 a year in direct federal financial support—a portion of which came from the National Endowment of the Arts.

The discovery that this type of offensive work was being funded by the federal government prompted more than fifty members of the Senate and House to sign a letter of protest to the National Endowment, which distributes $170 million each year.

The eventual cancellation of the art show intensified charges of censorship.

From the campus of UCLA came more accusations of censorship. A sixteen-minute film made by a university student, entitled "Animal Attractions," was screened at the institution as part of a week-long film festival. The film graphically depicted bestiality. About sixty protestors demonstrated against the film. The chancellor condemned the movie as "offensive, tasteless and disgusting," and said it would not be shown on campus again. The chancellor added, however, that the film was not censored because it was not legally pornographic.

To avoid pleas of "censorship" and judicial confusion, the Miller Standard must be envoked. Judges, chancellors, and politicians cannot be permitted to say "their hands are tied." Current ambiguities in the law permit and encourage officials to wash their hands of the pornographic problem polluting society.

"SAY IT AIN'T SO..."

Sporting events monopolize millions of television sets. Consequently, amateur and professional athletes have become the real-life actors in an unscripted soap opera. And like Hollywood celebrities, the off-screen antics of athletes have become newsworthy. Sometimes, when the news is negative, it has an adverse effect on the many children who idolize and emulate sports heroes.

Babe Ruth, who belted more than seven hundred home runs, was the most prolific player of his day. Americans clamored for his autograph or friendly handshake. On the field, no one could compete with his home run power and flare for the spectacular. Off the diamond, rumors of his abuse of alcohol, fist fights, and "wild revelry" were rampant. His behavior prompted New York City Mayor Jimmy Walker to chastise the slugger: "You're letting down all the dirty faced kids in the streets who love you."

Ruth's marriage was falling apart and a relationship with another woman was blossoming. The press was aware of Ruth's secret love, but chose to keep it out of the papers. Perhaps the press felt it was not newsworthy; or maybe they had reservations about disillusioning the young people of America who worshiped the ballplayer. The public relations efforts to uphold Ruth's philanthropic, compassionate image were brilliantly engineered. That is not to infer necessarily that Ruth was not a generous, caring man; it merely means the Yankees went to great lengths to publicize his good deeds to counteract the less-favorable impressions Ruth had left in his wake.

Pundits insist athletes have always led lives that were less than saintly; but in years past what occurred away from the sports arena often remained unreported. The press left the private lives of athletes private. Save the 1919 "Black Sox" scandal, when the Chicago White Sox allegedly threw the World Series, many reporters have repeatedly chosen to protect sports celebrities. Peter Alfano, in the New York Times, concurred:

> Contract troubles are not new in sports. Neither is animosity among teammates, petty jealousies, womanizing or drinking. Drugs are identified with this generation of athletes, but alcohol has probably destroyed or prematurely ended more careers than cocaine. The difference is that jour-

nalists no longer protect athletes as role models and heroes. We expose their warts as well as celebrate their exploits. They have become all too human.[6]

In more recent years, the personal episodes of athletes have been reported... and not confined to the sports page either. They've become front page news and lead stories on televsion newscasts.

Steve Howe was touted as one of the finest young pitchers in baseball after being named Rookie of the Year in 1980. Three years later, due to cocaine abuse, the Los Angeles Dodger southpaw was fined $54,000 and suspended for the 1984 season by then Commissioner Bowie Kuhn. The years following, Howe bounced between ballclubs, allegedly still battling a cocaine habit. The stirring story of his fall from stardom was widely chronicled; fans around the country shook their heads in disbelief.

In 1988, it was reported that Boston Red Sox third baseman Wade Boggs had entered into an adulterous relationship with Margo Adams. The particulars of the seedy affair were unveiled for the nation to read day after day. Adams filed a palimony lawsuit, requesting $6 million from Boggs.

Potential Hall of Famer and former manager of the Cincinnati Reds, Pete Rose, was catapulted into the spotlight in 1989 when it was reported that he had a gambling problem. A special investigator's inquiry accused Rose of betting on major league baseball, including the Cincinnati Reds. Though never corroborated, there were also allegations of drug dealing and tax evasion. The story grew darker for Pete Rose as more details came public; finally Rose agreed to accept then Commissioner Bart

Giamatti's banishment from baseball. Nonetheless, in the face of mounting evidence against him, Rose maintained his innocence. At one time known as the larger than life hero "Charlie Hustle," who epitomized dedication and effort, Rose was lowered to a mere mortal in the eyes of his fans.

Other sports have also been affected by revelations of impropriety and immorality. Both the National Basketball Association and National Football League have had to enforce their share of violations to drug policies. And the NCAA has had to suspend athletes and put entire sports programs on probation at an unparalleled rate. During the course of several months, at the University of Oklahoma, three football players were arraigned for attempted rape, another was arrested for shooting a fellow student, and a fifth athlete was sentenced for dealing cocaine.

Society has placed such a premium on success, that to attain it, some coaches have turned to cheating and some athletes have turned to drugs. Apparently, experiencing the joy of competition, building character, and developing sportsmanship are no longer worthy goals. For many professional athletes, success means stardom, financial security, and unrestrained liberties. College and high school athletes across the country are aspiring to become professionals so they can reap financial rewards and accolades as well. Many, unfortunately, are paying too great a price. Sports and many other forms of entertainment—when taken to extremes—have played a part in the secularization of America by detracting attention from faith in God and placing it on things which are temporal and satisfying to the flesh.

Young people and adults alike must realize that athletes are fallible. And the liberal lifestlyes some enjoy and the secularistic philosophies some espouse are not always worthy of being emulated.

SIX

NEWS MEDIA: A WEALTH OF MISINFORMATION

Two things I read every morning before I get
started: my Bible and the *New York Times* so I
know what each side is doing.
                   —Cal Thomas

In 1776 one half of the literature in America was
religious or published by religious groups. Many printers
specialized in printing Bibles, although Colonial printers
did not produce a complete English Bible until 1782. By
1800 there were 180 newspapers in the colonies. Many of
the major newspapers were characterized by a Christian
world view. Historians, nonetheless, have ignored the
findings of men like Marvin Olasky, who, in his book
Prodigal Press, said that in the early nineteenth century
"Of all the reading of the people, three-fourths is

127

religious...of all the issues of the press three-fourths are theological, ethical and devotional." Between 1825 and 1845, more than "one hundred cities and towns had explicitly Christian newspapers."

Christian newspapers did not limit their reporting to the theological; they reported and commented on matters relevant to daily life. According to Olasky, "aggressive journalism by Christians disappeared" because: newspapers began to ignore evil and thereby eventually became tolerant of it; they began to focus on positive news; they "refused to meet the communication demands of an increasingly fast-paced market"; and, lastly, they devoted too much time and space to denominational infighting. Olasky wrote, "During the last two-thirds of the nineteenth century, American society generally was casting aside the Christian principles on which it had been founded. Every area of American life [including the media] was affected by this shift."

DATELINE TENNESSEE

More than one hundred reporters rushed to Dayton, Tennessee to cover the trial of science teacher John Scopes. The reporters themselves and the articles they filed overwhelmingly favored evolution. Creationists were depicted as uncultured, unlearned zealots and Scopes was portrayed as an "imprisoned victim." The prosecuting attorney, William Jennings Bryan, was labeled inept and members of the jury were attacked for their church attendance.

Renowned columnist and author H.L. Mencken slurred Christians when he wrote, "On the one side was bigotry, ignorance, hatred, superstition, every sort of blackness that the human mind is capable of. On the other side was sense." In his obituary of Bryan, Mencken wrote, "...This talk of sincerity, I confess, fatigues me. If the fellow was sincere, then so was P.T. Barnum.... He was, in fact, a charlatan, a mountebank, a zany without shame or dignity." In 1926, Walter Lippmann lauded Mencken as "the most powerful personal influence on this whole generation of educated people." Six decades later Bryan's accuser became the accused... as Mencken's diary was released to the public. It exposed the revered journalist as anti-semitic, racist and pro-Nazi. Mencken—the charlatan, the hypocrite—used the influence of his pen to crucify Bryan and tilt public opinion. Yet, there were few, if any, written responses to Mencken's editorials opposing Bryan and Christianity, for by this time believers were no longer in prominent positions on newspaper staffs.

The media onslaught against Bryan diminished his place in history. But as stated in Wayne C. Williams' book, *Bryan—a Study in Political Vindication*, "No other man in American public life has ever lived to see so many of his ideas and reforms accepted by his political opponents and the people at large and established in the fundamental law and institutions of the land."

NEWSPAPER TYCOONS

Olasky made an astute observation when he wrote: "There is little evidence of editors explicitly banning God from the front page. Instead, they redefined 'reality' to exclude the spiritual realm.... But many editors of the past century have tried to publish God's obituary." Olasky pointed to such editors as Horace Greely of the *New York Tribune*, Wilbur Storey of the *Detroit Free Press* and *Chicago Times*, and E.W. Howe as men who used their influential positions in the newspaper world to secularize their vast readership. But their influence is trivial when compared to publishers Joseph Pulitzer, E.W. Scripps, and William Randolph Hearst.

Pulitzer's life was marked by newspaper genius and inner turmoil. He could build a newspaper empire and could run it like a tyrant, but he had difficulty governing his personal affairs. The complexity of dealing with his inner conflicts and his denial of the existence of a caring God led him to the brink of self-destruction. This theology manifested itself in his newspapers. The papers dealt with the sensational, lending few inches of copy to anything favoring Christianity.

"Scripps also extended the Greely-Pulitzer concept of newspapers as voices of the theological and political left," said Olasky. Scripps said of himself, "I do not believe in God, or any being equal to or similar to the Christian's God." He was a socialist who openly advocated revolution in his papers' editorials.

Hearst used his newspaper chain's influence to accomplish several objectives: to build a financial dynasty, to exalt himself, to promote his ideology, and to destroy his enemies. He had a list of two thousand persons who were to be mentioned "only with scorn" in his newspapers.

The publishers and corporate boards which own today's larger newspapers no longer have outright control of the editorial content or reporting. News editors and reporters have a greater say in what appears in print. Although secularists contend the majority of publishers are conservatives, the power of the pen lies in the hands of the overwhelmingly liberal news staffs—those who make the day-to-day editorial decisions.

A LIBERAL PRESS

A survey of 240 journalists from leading news departments was conducted by social scientists Stanley Rothman of Smith College and Robert Lichter of George Washington University. It revealed:

The majority of editors are politically left of center; only one in five categorizes himself as a conservative; they are predominantly Democrat. In 1972, 81 percent voted for George McGovern while 62 percent of the voters nationwide preferred Richard Nixon. (The 1976 election had similar results); half had no religious preference and 86 percent said they rarely attended religious services; the majority believe free enterprise does not give women an equal opportunity; most agree that American exploitation has contributed to Third World poverty and that the primary goal in U.S. foreign policy is to protect American business interests; and they oppose state ownership of major corporations, the sale of U.S. arms to foreign countries, and governmental involvement in a person's sexual practices.[1]

A *Los Angeles Times* poll, conducted in 1985, concluded that 55 percent of newspaper journalists consider themselves liberal. In contrast, only 24 percent of their readers are of that persuasion.

The primary question that must be answered deals with whether reporters' biases creep into their reporting. The answer is unequivocally "yes." Absolute objectivity in news reporting is impossible. When reporters write stories with opposing factions or views, they must decide which quotes are used and which receive prominence within the article. They must decide which participants to interview, which questions to ask, and which leads to explore. On occasion, a reporter bases these decisions on his or her bias. What is referred to as "sloppy" journalism is in some cases calculated, deceptive editorializing.

For an article which appeared in the *Los Angeles Times*, David Shaw interviewed editors to see whether they were satisfied with the job done by reporters when writing stories which involve their newspaper. David Kraslow, publisher of the *Miami News*, said, "When I contrast what I read in the paper with what I know to be the case from the inside...the kind of reportage we occasionally get is troublesome.... [There is] a lack of completeness, lack of balance, outright error...carelessness." Bill Kovach, editor of *The Atlanta Journal and Constitution*, told Shaw, "The strongest impression I have is the extent to which reporters arrive in my office [to interview me] with a preconceived notion of the story they're going to write. The interview is based primarily on the effort to elicit information and response that fits into that story line."

A public opinion survey released by the Times Mirror Center for People and the Press found in 1989 that public confidence in the American news industry is low. Only 28 percent of those polled felt news organizations "deal fairly with all sides"; 44 percent believed the news is "often inaccurate." If this poll is any indication, perhaps more people than journalists would like to believe concur with Edward R. Morrow's definition of local news: "A curious mixture of show business, carnival huckstering and journalism."

IGNORANCE AND THE LIBERAL AGENDA

Most news staffs are comprised of unchurched reporters. A *Los Angeles Times* article entitled "Media View Religion in a News Light" by staff writer Shaw addressed this point, saying:

> Fewer than 200 of the nation's more than 1,700 daily newspapers have religion writers, and only about a third of these 200 cover religion full-time. Although some of these full-time religion writers do consistently excellent work, most religion stories that appear in the nation's newspapers are written by general assignment reporters, political reporters, feature writers or others with little understanding of—or interest in—religion.... Most newspapers [twenty years ago] assigned their church page duties to their oldest over-the-hill reporters or to the staff alcoholic or, most often, to their youngest, least experienced reporters.

When it comes to reporting on theological issues or basic Judeo-Christian principles, most journalists must plead ignorance. But ignorance is only part of the issue. Some reporters, consciously and subconsciously, slight Christianity because they have their own ideological agenda. They camouflage their secular concepts in the rags of objectivity and fair reporting, though in reality it is calculated ideological propaganda in its truest form.

In the early days of journalism, reporters were less secretive with their biases. Their opinions were easily interpreted from their news articles. In some respects, that made it easier on readers, for they were not having to deal with disinformation hidden in the cloak of objectivity.

133

The New York Times, for example, in 1871, left no doubt of its opinion on abortion when it printed the headline "The Evil of This Age." The news article said, "Thousands of human beings are murdered before they have seen the light of this world, and thousands upon thousands more adults are irremediably robbed in constitution, health and happiness."

The reporting today still contains biases, only it is more difficult to determine what information is factual and what is opinion. At a pro-abortion rally in Washington, D.C., the *Los Angeles Herald* reported that 600,000 protesters marched to the capital. A television station reported 700,000. Police, meanwhile, reported there were only 300,000 in attendance. More discrepancies occurred surrounding the marches **against** the screening of *The Last Temptation of Christ,* but this time the reported attendance figures were much lower than police records.

Turner Broadcasting president and Cable News Network founder Ted Turner—who said "Christianity is a religion for losers"—chose to telecast an "explicit video that unquestionably endorses legalized abortion." The production, "Abortion: For Survival," was produced by the Fund for Feminist Majority. Turner defended his decision to air the video: "You bet your bippy we're taking a position. I don't want anybody else telling me what my daughter's got to have, or my wife, or my girlfriend. We live in a free country."

When the press does cover religious topics, it usually deals with the "sensational, superficial, scandalous or stereotypical.... But in covering religion, the press often seems obsessed with conflict, controversy and...trivial personality stories," wrote Shaw.

George Cornell of the Associated Press said, "...there

is very little in the American press about how religion actually influences people's daily lives."

Polls continue to show that a large percentage of Americans hold an interest in spiritual matters. Nonetheless, as Shaw noted, "...there has been little detailed press coverage of this increased religiosity. Nor has the press spent much time examining the seeming contradiction between this increase and the concomitant shift away from traditional denominations and, among some people, away from religion itself."

Robert Bellah, professor of Sociology, said, "Most journalists are simply blind to religion. They think its'somehow slightly embarrassing, a holdover from the Dark Ages...something only ignorant and backward people really believe in."

Perhaps not much has changed since the Scopes Trial after all.

AN UNRESTRAINED PRESS

Alexander Solzhenitsyn said:

> The press has become the greatest power within the Western countries, exceeding that of the legislature, the executive, and the judiciary.... Unrestrained freedom exists for the press, but not for the readership, because newspapers mostly transmit in a forceful and emphatic way those opinions which do not too openly contradict their own and that general trend.

A liberal press which has unlimited power and privilege is like a pack of wild broncos. The liberties now enjoyed by members of the press were granted by the courts. The *New York Times* v. *Sullivan* Supreme Court decision in 1964 was certainly a landmark case. It gave the press the freedom to print what it wanted about a public person without fear of being held accountable. A public person—though he may suffer defamation by a report—could not sue for punitive damages unless he could prove a statement "was false, and that it was made with knowledge of its falsity or in reckless disregard of whether it was false or true."

Prior to this decision, printing the truth was ample defense against prosecution. Now, in many cases, "truth" is irrelevant to the courts. As a result, there has been an upsurge of "trash tabloids" like the *National Enquirer* which thrive on untruths and sensationalism with little regard for the facts or what harm may come to reputations. Some "journalists" continue to print the unsubstantiated, function with minimum accountability, and invade privacy.

The courts and society as a whole are beginning to recognize the dangers associated with an unbridled press. In 1989, the California Supreme Court ruled that "private individuals can sue for libel even if a story that defames them with false information is published without malice and in the public interest." Needless to say, there have been the usual cries of censorship, accusations that the First Amendment right of freedom of the press has been abridged. But society's demand for responsible journalism is far from demanding censorship. And the Christian plea for fairness and equal time is far from seeking to control the press.

As David Shaw wrote, "... the press could be the best vehicle for furthering religious understanding and tolerance in our society."

SEVEN

FAMILY: UNDER THE INFLUENCE

The American family does not exist. Rather, we are creating many American families, of diverse styles and shapes.
—*Newsweek*, 1989

One of the most appalling signs of a secularized society is its disrespect for the traditional family unit. A myriad of forces and shifting values have led to this dangerous restructuring of the American home. The upsurge of divorce, domestic violence, addictions, government intrusion into the home, secular education, and abortion are among the most dominant factors leading to the decay of the family. This erosion has only perpetuated other societal problems. Once, the family unit was a pillar of democratic life; without it, democracy itself is in jeopardy. Certainly, the family as prescribed in Scripture is facing its toughest test since the nation's inception.

THE COLONIAL FAMILY

The founding fathers did not mention the family in the Declaration of Independence or the U.S. Constitution because they took it for granted that Americans would never neglect or dismantle such an esteemed part of their heritage.

William V. D'Antonio said, in his book *Family and Religion*:

> Since earliest times in the West, father has been 'boss,' and mother and children have been subordinate.... The interests of the family as a group took precedence over those of its individual members.... We gain our membership in the family by the mere fact of birth; we do not have to earn it.... It is increasingly perceived as the source of nurturance, love and affection.[1]

To the dismay of many, all this is changing.

Newsweek reported, "From Colonial days to the mid-19th century, most fathers and mothers worked side by side, in or near their homes, farming or plying trades. Each contributed to family income, and—within carefully delineated roles—they shared the responsibility of child rearing."

With the birth of the Industrial Revolution in the late 1800s, husbands delegated many of their home chores to their wife to go work in the factories. But this change in the family makeup, nor wars, nor the crusade for women's rights, nor the Great Depression, served to diminish respect or concern for the family unit. It survived unscathed.

The family crisis in America is a phenomena three decades old, when the '60s generation rebelled against parental authority. Since then other aspects of the traditional family unit have been methodically "overthrown" and discarded by a secular society.

DEMISE OF THE BIBLICAL FAMILY

In a poll conducted by the Gallup Organization and published in·*Newsweek*, half the adults surveyed felt the family is "worse off" then it was ten years ago. Half also said they believe the family will be "worse" yet ten years from now.

There is a reason for this pessimism, for life in the typical American home is in chaos, partly because the makeup of the family unit itself is in a state of flux. Ozzie and Harriet-like families are no longer the norm. D'Antonio wrote, "Only 30 percent of all families are fully nuclear in the sense of having husband, wife and children under one roof." Columnist George Will reported, "In 1988, 24 percent of America's 63 million children lived with only one parent, double the 1970 percentage. Most single-parent households are headed by women.... Only 39 percent of the children born in 1988 will live with both parents until their 18th birthday."

Newsweek said: "We have...fathers and mothers both working...; single parents; second marriages bringing children together from unrelated backgrounds; childless couples; unmarried couples, with and without children; and gay and lesbian parents."

Of the women comprising the work force, more than half are married. Thus, many of their "latchkey kids" are left to fend for themselves after school, which sometimes carries with it disheartening long term implications in the life of the child.

Marriage rates since the 1920s have remained constant, while the rate of divorce has tripled. D'Antonio found that "until 1970, divorce laws in the United States were very straight. Indeed, they had not changed much since 1890, when there were few divorces.... Divorce law was changed to reflect different behavior, not to cause it. And, as a result, the law was brought into greater conformity with values like freedom and equality."

Liberal divorce laws, though reflecting society's changing value system, have certainly made divorce easier and more acceptable. D'Antonio said:

> In traditional society, divorce was seen as a violation of sacred rules, and especially as a threat to community solidarity. A group bond was being broken. Now the values focus on the individual and the right to personal happiness. Divorce is recognition of the failure of a couple to establish or maintain a worthwhile, reciprocal relationship. An unhappy married person demands freedom to dissolve the marriage.[2]

One of the primary causes of divorce has always been adultery. Now the traditional belief that monogamy is dutiful is being denied on television and in the classroom. The ACLU, for example, wrote to members of California's Assembly Education Committee complaining it was "unconstitutional to teach that monogamous, heterosexual intercourse within marriage is a traditional American value."

Some married couples are deciding against having

children for economic reasons; and other couples are planning to have families out of wedlock. But perhaps the changing makeup of the family is epitomized by the growing number of gay and lesbian couples parenting children. One homosexual who is raising a child with another man said, "Our [he and his lover] values really are the same as those of our parents. We just happen to be two men." The man's lover added, "We're Ozzie and Harry."

It was reported by the Associated Press that a lesbian couple had won the right to adopt a two-year-old boy. An attorney for the couple denounced a prevalent state policy which prohibits unmarried couples from adopting children. He said, "Millie and Sue's marital status does not determine their parenting abilities." One of the lesbian "parents" said, "I'm 'Mommy;' she's 'Mama,' and it's really cute when he says, 'Mommy, Mama,' when he wants both of us."

Some lesbians are having their own children through insemination. In fact, one-third of the clients at the Feminist Women's Health Center in Atlanta are lesbians, having come there to be inseminated.

The very definition of "family" is being rewritten by a politically-aggressive gay community. The Massachusetts Mutual Life Insurance Company polled twelve hundred adults at random, asking them to define "family." "Only 22 percent gave the legalistic definition: 'a group of people related by blood, marriage or adoption." Almost 75 percent said the family is "a group of people who love and care for each other."

This new definition is maneuvering its way into our lawbooks. In New York, for instance, the Court of Appeals ruled that gay couples were the legal equivalent of a family. And in California, several cities have attempted to bestow rights to homosexual "partners" previously reserved for married couples.

In San Francisco, the Board of Supervisors voted unanimously for a "domestic partner" ordinance designed to recognize as a family "two people who have chosen to share one another's lives in an intimate and committed relationship." This would have given them some rights granted to married couples, including hospital and visitation rights and health insurance coverage. More than twenty-seven thousand signatures were solicited to overturn the ordinance. Shortly thereafter, the measure was defeated in a city-wide election.

Currently, the gay and lesbian community is endeavoring to change laws in all fifty states which do not allow individuals of the same sex to marry. An attorney for a gay rights organization wrote in the *New York Times*:

> Those who argue against reforming the marriage statutes because they believe that same sex marriage would be anti-family overlook the obvious: marriage creates families and promotes social stability. In an increasingly loveless world, those who wish to commit themselves to a relationship founded upon devotion should be encouraged, not scorned. Government has no legitimate interest in how that love is expressed.... Depriving millions of gay American adults the marriages of their choice, and the rights that flow from marriage, denies equal protection of the law. They, their families and friends, together with fair-minded people everywhere, should demand an end to this monstrous injustice.[3]

Gay activists are using a "moral" argument to justify and advocate an immoral lifestyle. They are attempting to persuade people to deny their traditionally-held belief— that marriage is meant for heterosexual relationships— by resorting to cries of discrimination. Unfortunately, more and more Americans are listening and, subsequently, agreeing that there should be no "discrimination" based on sexual-orientation. This is not an issue of discrimination; rather, it is an unfounded attempt to defy the traditional-biblical version of the family which has been the basis of western civilization.

A MIND OF THEIR OWN

Judeo-Christian values are not taught in many homes. Consequently, the values which **are** being assimilated by the youth of America cause many to worry about the future of the nation. In a survey of 1,093 high school seniors, 59 percent said they might risk six months on probation to pursue an "illegal" business deal worth $10 million. About 36 percent said they "would plagiarize in order to pass a certification test"; more than 50 percent said they "would inflate business expense reports,... exaggerate on an insurance damage report," and "lie to achieve a business objective."

This is typical of what a number of child psychologists and educators are calling a new phenomena: "Me-firstism." Stanford Psychologist Carl Thoresen said, "They're [children] highly competitive at very young ages. They can't work in groups, they're self-centered and selfish. And they tend to have the attitude that if you're not center stage, you're nothing."

The new selfishness, educators say, transcends the normal self-centered behavior of children seen in the past. The mentors of this learned behavior are parents and television. Said Thoreson, "The more self-focused the parent, the more self-focused the child." Psychiatrist Barbara Ferguson said, "Parents are far too pressured to sit back and assess their values and think about what they want to communicate to their children."

Television—the babysitter of the modern era—has also perpetuated a "Me-first" philosophy. As children increase their viewing hours and network officials provide irresponsible programming, a "brainwashing" of sorts takes place. Children tend to emulate their self-centered television heroes and seek advertisers' distorted view of "success."

The dangers of a generation of selfish thinkers are obvious, but, in particular, this attitude is detrimental to families. Personal interests, success, and achievement often take precedence over family unity, tenderness, togetherness, the common good, and family responsibility.

Some parents tend to devote far more attention to the child's accomplishments, or lack thereof, than they do to the demonstration of their unconditional love and affection. This has caused some children to leave the "nest" prematurely; every year one million teenagers run away from home.

"Parents should instill the values of service, connection to something better and greater than themselves, and reward expressions of love and cooperation, instead of winning and being first," said Larry Scherwitz, an assistant professor of behavior science.

The family is a microcosm of society. Without a Judeo-Christian ethic, the unit often experiences inner-turmoil.

DRUG AND ALCOHOL ABUSE

Many young people are venting their disgust with their family life through the use of drugs and alcohol. A study of junior high school students found that 40 percent used beer and nearly 30 percent indulged regularly in liquor.

William Bennett, once the Bush administration's drug czar, pledged a war on drugs that he hopes will result in a 50 percent reduction in drug and alcohol consumption before the twenty-first century. A major emphasis of this plan is to bolster educational efforts. But some experts have concluded that drug abuse is a symptom of a larger problem: the demise of the family unit. Others suggest drug use is merely a cause of family disintegration. In either case, more attention must be directed to keeping families together and combatting those influences and secularistic values which seek to devour the traditional family.

Drugs—especially cocaine—left families ravaged in the 1980s. Addicts are frequently so embroiled in their habit that eventually it takes a toll on their marriage and children. The family self-destructs, leaving grandparents to pick up the pieces—the children abandoned by addicted parents. More and more, however, the children of addicts are being turned over to the state to be sent to orphanages or foster homes where they frequently have to wrestle with feelings of guilt and inferiority. They grow up without parental affection and values training. Many of them also turn to drugs to mask their own emotional scars.

Alcohol and cocaine have become temptations to every segment of society. No race, age group, or extended family is isolated from their tentacles.

TEENAGE VIOLENCE

Nine persons in New York were randomly assaulted by thirty-two youths in 1989. The news prompted First Lady Barbara Bush to say, "People are going to have to reevaluate their lives and put their children first.... Life is too fast, and it's tough on family life."

USA Today reported that eight boys—ranging in ages thirteen to seventeen—were accused of ambushing a woman in New York's Central Park. The attack was allegedly part of a "wilding spree," where a pack of teenagers vented their frustration and boredom with a violent rampage. The teens displayed no remorse for their alleged crime. "It was fun," said one of the suspected attackers.

Richard Cloward, social work professor, believes there is going to be an increase in this peer-pressure-induced teenage violence: "Many of these kids sense no one cares about them, and often they're not wrong."

Children who feel alone will find or form their own family—even if they have to surround themselves with criminals or malcontents.

SUICIDE

"The three leading causes of death among adolescents are drug and alcohol-related accidents, suicide and homicide," wrote Susan Baker and Tipper Gore in their article "Some Reasons for Wilding," in *Newsweek* (May 29, 1989). Every year 600,000 teenagers attempt suicide and five thousand succeed. "There are many complex reasons for this sad litany. Divorce and working parents strain the family's ability to cope. Latchkey kids are the rule more than the exception. Our schools and neighborhoods have become open-air drug markets. But it is not enough to excuse these children as products of a bad environment.... The moral crisis facing our nation's youth requires that we all share the responsibility, parents and the entertainment industry."

BIG BROTHER BECOMES BIG DADDY

Organizations like Planned Parenthood, which indirectly receive funds from the government, have made a frontal assault on the family. By advocating abortions for teenagers without the need for parental consent, Planned Parenthood has, in effect, served to devalue the parent-child relationship. By the mere funding of such organizations the government is indirectly usurping parental rights.

Politicians and pro-abortionists have also proposed school-based clincs, from which students would receive contraceptives and counseling on abortion and sex-related matters. Again, this is an attempt by liberals to usurp a parent's right to discuss private matters with his or her child.

The ABC Childcare Bill is another effort by the government to meddle in the affairs of the family. The bill proposed that government oversee a national child care program. Centers that pray before snack times, tell Bible stories, have crosses on their buildings, or have any religious conotation would not qualify for this new federal aid because of "separation of church and state." Without this aid, Christian-run centers would not be able to compete with secular centers that would gladly comply with the government's requirements.

Nearly 40 percent of the voting public expressed dissatisfaction with their child care, according to a poll conducted in 1989. Thus, liberal politicians seized the opportunity to introduce legislation which would virtually extend and escalate the secularistic indoctrination of the young sought by educators like John Dewey and Horace Mann. The ABC Childcare package, if passed, would allow the government to determine what can be taught in day care centers across the land.

Because child care benefits would only be given to parents who use government-licensed centers, the bill is discriminatory against parents who would choose to care for their own children or seek other avenues of care. In effect, through a subtle form of economic blackmail, the government would be dictating to parents where their children receive day care.

Pro-family activist Phyllis Schlafly said:

The original Dodd ABC day care bill...contained some of the most virulently anti-religious language ever seen in any proposed legislation. The bill's advocates changed some of the language... but they did not diminish the problem at all. The problem is explained in a 12-page Department of Justice opinion...which concludes that the ABC bill would impose on all religious day care 'clear litigation risks' and 'oppressive government oversight.'

Currently, according to the U.S. Census Bureau, only 15 percent of the children under five years of age are cared for in day care centers while their mothers are at work. If the government becomes involved in the child care business, these percentages would rise dramatically, for many more working mothers would take advantage of the program. Government-run centers would invariably supplant church-run centers. And, no doubt, speaking about God, praying and reading the Bible would be eliminated from the centers' routine. Secular ideas would replace that which is biblical, for the government would dictate what is learned and what would be ignored.

Parents naturally fear their rights and the rights of the traditional family are being disregarded by the government, and the ABC bill is just one example.

Government leaders and social activists claim they are endeavoring to assist families in need by providing child care aid. In reality, under the guise of assistance, they are seeking to socialize and secularize. And in both cases the family is the loser.

EIGHT

HUMAN RIGHTS: COMPLIMENTS OF OUR CREATOR

> ... all men are created equal, that they are endowed by their Creator with certain inalienable rights.
>
> —Declaration of Independence

Central to the secular movement's quest for de-Christianization is a devaluation of the rights of the human fetus; equally important to their liberal cause is the elevation of rights of special interest groups such as homosexuals. Secularists, in practice, do not advocate equal rights; rather, they prefer to grant disproportionate privileges based on what is most advantageous to their philosophical goals.

Throughout history, societies which have denied the value of a single human life and distributed preferential treatment to specialized groups, have invariably experienced religious deterioration or spiritual drought. In this nation's brief history, its spiritual tenor has paralleled its appraisal of human life and support of equal rights.

AMERICAN SLAVERY

At the outbreak of the Revolutionary War, there were six thousand slaves in Massachusetts. Some religious denominations, including the Quakers, actively protested the practice of slavery as being contrary to God's Word. Later, other faiths would pass anti-slavery resolutions; and at one time it seemed slavery was on a course to abandonment. But all that changed with the invention of the cotton gin in 1792. Cotton soon became the most important product coming out of the South. Many were convinced that the nation's welfare rested on the success of the cotton industry. The profits from a plantation cotton crop were directly related to having cheap labor—slaves to work the fields. Thus, southern leaders favored slavery for economic reasons more than any ideological conviction.

Preachers in the north spoke fiercely against the denial of human rights in the South. Many ministers in the South, meanwhile, continued their claim that slavery was within the parameters of God's will. This led to denominational splits and infighting among cooperative congregations. The Reverend J.H. Thornwall of South Carolina said, "I cannot regard slavery as a moral evil.... It is distinctly recognized by Moses; it is not inconsistent with the precepts of Christianity."

In his book *The Peculiar Institution*, Kenneth Stampp said, "Christians...believed it just to hold heathens in servitude, and...found victims among the Negroes in

Africa.... The Christian purchasers liked to think of themselves as the agents of civilization and of the true religion."

In the name of evangelism and "civilizing" Africans, some Christian slave traders and slave owners justified their materialistic activities. They ignored the biblical message of equality and in doing so secularized the religion of the southern churches—at least as it pertained to human rights.

Arnold J. Toynbee, in *A Study of History*, wrote:

It is one thing, however, to possess a spiritual treasure and quite another thing to impart it; and, the more we think over it, the more astonishing we shall find it to be that these Christian slave-owners' hands should have been able to transmit to their primitive pagan victims the spiritual bread which they had done their best to desecrate by the sacrilegious act of enslaving their fellow-men. How could the slave- driver evangelist ever touch the heart of the slave whom he had morally alienated by doing him so grievous a wrong?[1]

In his comparative study of slavery and abortion, J.C. Willke quoted Lowell Dumond, author of *Anti-Slavery:*

Slavery was the complete subjugation by force of one person to the will of another recognized and sustained by state law. Slavery was the subordination of nearly four-million negroes to the status of beasts of the field, insofar as possible, in a nation dedicated to freedom and equality of all men. Slavery was a deadly virus which twisted and distorted intellectual processes, social attitudes, and religious philosophy. It contaminated everything it touched from the early Colonial days until 1865....[2]

The anti-slavery movement gained new momentum during the 1830s despite deeply rooted indoctrination which had taken place in the South. During this period, said Willke:

[A great] Christian revival gave the anti-slavery movement an uncounted number of devoted apostles. In particular, the Presbyterian and Congregational Churches provided forums for these men, who brought great power to the movement because of their numbers, their organization, and their following of the Bible. All of this was needed to beat down and destroy the doctrine of racial inequality and the enshrinement of slavery, tragically upheld by so many churches.[3]

The verbal war over slavery would eventually result in Civil War, 1861-1865. President Abraham Lincoln took the lead in the anti-slavery movement. He preached: "...nothing stamped with the Divine image and likeness was sent into the world to be trodden on, and degraded, and imbruted by its fellows. They grasped not only the whole race of man then living, but they reached forward and seized upon the farthest posterity."

Despite presidential leadership on the issue, biographer Elton Trueblood maintained that Lincoln was not completely successful in rallying Christians against slavery: "Lincoln was impatient with Christian organizations which could not unite in opposition to something as obvious as the sinfulness of human slavery."

Churches of the North provided education and religious instruction for former slaves they had helped remove from slavery's snare. On the other hand, the churches which wallowed in apathy and those which propagated slavery also left their mark on society. By denying or not proclaiming that according to God's Word all men were created equal, they allowed ungodly practices to pervade society and were thereby accomplices in the quest to secularize it.

THE PLIGHT OF INDIANS

Slave raids of tribal lands started shortly after Spanish explorers came to North America. The "heathen" Indians were "considered the foes of Christ" and were treated accordingly by the Spanish settlers. Many Indians were killed, maimed, and separated from their families.

L.R. Bailey's book, *Indian Slave Trade in the Southwest*, noted, "Indeed, the policy of slave raiding existed side-by-side with the [Spanish] missionary effort, and worked much to the detriment of the latter." Between 1700 and 1760, nearly eight hundred Apache Indians were forcibly anointed with oil and baptized into Catholicism. Despite their new religion, they remained servants and "menials."

As the United States expanded its western borders, the nation inherited land which reeked with the highly-profitable Indian slave-trade business. Bailey said:

> ...Indian groups—those bearing the brunt of slave raiding—were pushed from their traditional lands, onto and against still other Indian groups, or into closer contact with white men—and this oscilla-

tion produced flarings of warfare which kept the southwest in turmoil for generations.... There is every reason to believe that the trade in chattel was at its height from 1846 to the outbreak of the Civil War. Many American military commanders, like their Spanish and Mexican counterparts, either aided and abetted this nefarious practice or closed their eyes to it.... And many petty politicians maintained their strength and popularity by pandering to the whims of slave procurers....[4]

Finally, the U.S. government took steps to protect Indians and provide them with reservation territories. Nonetheless, respect for the rights of these tribes was lacking within American culture. Indians were perceived as a hinderance to progressive American society. And although some missionaries jeopardized their lives to share the gospel with them, for the most part, tribes were decimated and stripped of their land while the Church remained silent.

During this era, society's respect for all human life and equal opportunity was subdued at best.

WOMEN'S RIGHTS

The feminists of the modern era are not carrying the same torch for equal rights championed by their nineteenth century predecessors. The women's movement of the 1840s involved Christians who believed "the woman is man's equal—was intended to be so by the Creator, and the highest good of the race demands that she should be recognized as such." In 1848, women of all ages attended a convention in Seneca Falls, New York to discuss the "social, civil and religious conditions and rights of women...." The convention's attendees drew up a "Declaration of Sentiments and Resolutions" which called for the right to vote and own property, equal protection in divorce proceedings, equal remuneration from employers, equal opportunities, and a role within the church.

In the 1870s, thousands of women belonging to the Women's Christian Temperance Union (WCTU) marched in protest of alcohol. But the organization did more than fight to eliminate alcohol abuse, according to Ruth Bordin's book *Woman and Temperance*: [It] "worked toward the right to vote for women, prison reform, facilities for dependent and neglected children, and federal aid to education. Originally acting through church networks, the Union eventually adopted legislation and political means to try to bring about change."

Even though the WCTU became "a model for future women's organizations" and was the largest organization of women the United States had yet known (150,000 dues paying members), it has received little notoriety from historians. During its heyday the Union was successful in getting temperance education legislation passed and rallying public support for prohibition. The successes of the organization can be linked to the numerous missionary societies and Protestant denominations which were converted into WCTU chapters. "...the WCTU was certainly church-oriented, and almost all of its members were church-going Protestants," said Bordin.

Today's feminist movement in no way proliferates biblical, pro-family values as did the WCTU and similar women's groups. Instead, it advances secular ideals detrimental to the traditional family.

In the 1970s and 1980s the Equal Rights Amendment was a rallying cause for the feminist movement. The ERA was defeated, however, when it was not ratified by the prescribed number of states. Critics of the amendment said the legislation was unnecessary because women already have equal rights protection under the U.S. Constitution.

Homemakers, in particular, proved to be skeptical of the ERA. They felt they were being asked as writer Deborah Rhode reported, "to relinquish tangible benefits in exchange for a vague promise of dubious value." Furthermore, said author Jane Mansbridge in *Why We Lost the ERA*, "From the beginning of the modern women's movement in the mid-1960s, feminists had been ideologically opposed to, or at best ambivalent about, homemaking as a full-time career. In turn, homemakers had been ideologically opposed to...important planks in the feminist platform." They, by and large, were also not in agreement with the position taken by the National Organization for Women (NOW) favoring interracial marriage, abortion, and homosexuality.

The defeat of the ERA in the 1980s, NOW's militant approach, and secular philosophy have resulted in significant defections from the movement. And when NOW called for the creation of a third political party, desertion among the group's 220,000 members intensified.

Considered the nation's major women's organization since its inception in 1966, NOW's liberal leaders are often quoted as if they were representing the views of the majority of women in America. Little attention is given to more conservative groups such as Concerned Women of America (CWA), founded in 1979, which boasts a membership of 600,000.

CWA founder and President Beverly LaHaye represented the views of her constituency when she said, "We felt that the wording of the ERA was too vague. It could absolutely get out of control.... We felt that women were going to be hurt and families were going to be hurt by [the] ERA, and so we were campaigning against it vigorously."

BLACK CIVIL RIGHTS

In 1934, during his weekly Sunday evening radio broadcast on NBC, Will Rogers used the word "nigger" four times. The cowboy-comedian and NBC refused to apologize. According to an editor connected with the program, the network could not interfere with Rogers' show for fear of violating his First Amendment rights. Blacks threatened to boycott NBC and all products manufactured by the Gulf Refining Company, which owned the network. Consequently, the following week the comedian substituted the word "darky" when referring to a Black American.

In subsequent years Blacks would face more humiliation, segregation, discrimination, and imposed poverty. Then Martin Luther King, Jr., a Baptist minister, burst on the scene like Moses coming to set his people free. King effectively employed his pulpit and a network of Black churches in the struggle for equal rights.

Some Caucasian churches and leaders joined King in his crusade. But, as in the prejudicial days of the Civil War and the Wild West, many churches rested in quietude. Many Christians were content to watch Blacks endure oppression. The society which refused to uphold equal rights for every race, had in reality devalued human life, disobeyed the Bible, and denied the beauty of God's creation.

King, meanwhile, appealed to Scripture to prepare

his troops for non-violent confrontation: "Our actions must be guided by the deepest principles of the Christian faith.... Once again we must hear the words of Jesus, 'Love your enemies. Bless them that curse you. Pray for them that despitefully use you.'"

Segregation would also have a de-Christianizing effect on society, for in practicing discrimination man was disobeying Scripture. King said:

> What we are doing is not only for the black man, but for the white man too. The system that has banished personality and scarred the soul of the Negro has also damaged the white man's personality, giving him a false sense of superiority as it gives the Negro a false sense of inferiority. Segregation is as bad for one as for the other. So in freeing the Negro we will also free the white man of his misconceptions and his subconscious feeling of guilt toward those he wrongs.

The Civil Rights Act of 1964 and the Voting Rights Bill of the following year represented a major advancement for the rights of Blacks. Further progress would be made subsequent to King's assassination in 1968, for then he would assume martyr status to the future generations who would carry on his dream.

Twenty years after the civil rights leader's death he is still being lauded as the father of Black freedom. For some, he has become more than a gifted leader; he has become immortal. Herein lies another danger prevalent in a secularized society—creating gods of men posthumously, and then manipulating their message once they are gone to fit a secular agenda.

LEGITIMIZING A LIFESTYLE

Gay rights proponents have likened their struggle for "equality" to the Black Civil Rights movement. But the analogy is far-fetched when one considers the obvious incongrueties. Blacks were seeking basic human rights: the right to vote, to reverse segregation laws, to receive equal opportunity. Homosexuals already enjoy these privileges; now they are seeking to go beyond equal rights to obtain "preferential" treatment. Under the banner of gaining "equal rights," gays and lesbians are seeking to form an elite sect for themselves based soley on their sexual orientation. As Alexander Solzhenitsyn said, "The defense of individual rights has reached such extremes as to make society as a whole defenseless against certain individuals. It is time, in the West, to defend not so much human rights as human obligations."

Homosexual leaders have also tried to equate an incident occurring at a bar in Greenwich Village to altercations between Blacks and police during the early 1960s. In 1969 the Stonewall Inn was raided by police. Following a confrontation, *Newsweek* said, "Drag queens, leather boys and assorted demimondaines" were hauled off to jail. The event received minimal recognition in the press but "within days, activists formed the Gay Liberation Front, one of the nations's first militantly homosexual organizations."

Massachusetts Representative Barney Frank said of the Stonewall incident, "Every movement has to have symbols that provide some common sense of history. It was an extraordinary event that was important contemporaneously and probably even more important since then." For gays, Stonewall proportedly marked "the coming out from behind closet doors."

Novelist Edmund White, who happened to be at Stonewall that night, said, "Up to Stonewall, the only possible definition for gays was that homosexuality was a sin, a crime or a disease. Suddenly, we were saying we were not any of those, but a minority group."

At one time, homosexuality was viewed by the American Psychiatric Association as a mental illness. That changed in 1973, and since then gays have gained significant public acceptance. A 1989 Gallup Poll found that 47 percent of Americans felt homosexual relations should be legalized, opposed to 36 percent who said it should not be. Two years earlier only 33 percent felt homosexuality should be permitted by law. More than 40 percent said it was appropriate for homosexuals to serve as high school and elementary teachers and in the clergy.

Segments of this secularized society—including many churches and clergymen—ignore Scriptures which unequivocally denounce homosexual relations.

To justify their decadent lifestyle in a religious setting, gays have formed their own churches—churches which do not embrace the Bible in its entirety. Some mainline churches and believers, nonetheless, have virtually condoned homosexuality; in doing so, they have allowed the movement to make inroads to mainstream society.

The movement's advancements are numerous. Homosexual organizations can be found on most university campuses; the first homosexual public high school was established; state-run AIDS education programs indirectly promote homosexuality; gay awareness days and parades are held in many cities; and anti-discrimination laws for gays provide them with special privileges.

Indicative of the progress made by the gay community is a case in Minneapolis. An applicant to the Big Brother organization admitted to an interviewer that he was homosexual. The interviewer in turn relayed this information to the mother of a boy with which the gay applicant was assigned to spend time. A court case ensued and the hearing officer determined it was illegal and discriminatory to tell the boy's mother of the Big Brother's sexual preference. *Citizen Magazine* reported that the organization was assessed $6,000 in costs and "...even more troubling was the officer's finding that the organization had to engage in 'affirmative action.' The action required Big Brothers to solicit homosexuals to be secret Big Brothers in Minneapolis by placing ads in homosexual magazines in Los Angeles and San Francisco."

Fortunately, the ruling was overturned by an apellate court. But as the barrage of cases escalates, secularists are nipping away at the consensus that homosexuality is indeed immoral.

WHEN A BABY BECAME A FETUS

Secularists have engaged in a war of semantics—an effort to redefine terminology as it pertains to human life.

Bill Nelson, host of "California Breeze," reported on his program that *Webster's Collegiate Dictionary, 1966*, defined "Aborticide": "to kill, destruction of the fetus in the womb." *Webster's Collegiate Dictionary, 1975*, had no listing or definition of the word.

Up until 1962 most newspapers used the word "baby" when describing an abortion. Today, with the influence of secular humanists, the child is merely a "fetus."

The American Medical Association (AMA) has altered its policy statements over the years to accommodate a secular view of human life. In 1859, abortion was defined by the AMA as "The slaughter of countless children; no mere misdemeanor, no attempt upon the life of the mother but the wanton and murderous destruction of her child; such unwarrantable destruction of human life." In 1871 abortion was still, according to the AMA, "The work of destruction; the wholesale destruction of unborn infants." But by 1970 abortion was "The interruption of an unwanted pregnancy.... A medical procedure."

The AMA also went on record in 1871, declaring:

> Thou shalt not kill; this commandment is given to all and applies to all without exception; it matters not at what stage of development his victim may have arrived—it matters not how small or how apparently insignificant it may be—it is murder, a foul, unprovoked murder, and its blood, like the blood of Abel, will cry from earth to Heaven for vengeance.

Up until recent years doctors took the Hypocratic Oath: "I will give no deadly medicine to anyone if asked, nor suggest such counsel, and in like manner, I will not give a woman a pessary to produce abortion." The new oath reads: "I will do nothing that is illegal."

The Planned Parenthood organization—founded as the American Birth Control League in 1917—has led the fight in the redefining of terms and the redrawing of legislation concerning abortion. Planned Parenthood's founder, Margaret Sanger, successfully garnered tax dollars and government support for some of her anti-biblical ideals. She maintained, said biographer Elasah Drogin, that the rationale for "limiting the amount of children for the poorer classes of people was that the human race—in order to survive—would have to purify its genetic treasury through the use of such methods as requiring parents to apply for licenses to have babies... and forcibly sterilizing poor people, while at the same time encouraging the more 'succesful' human types and races to beget more children...." Sanger summed up her philosophy when she said, "more children for the fit, less from the unfit—that is the chief aim of birth control." In her "Plan for Peace," published in her *Birth Control Review Magazine*, Sanger detailed a plan for peaceful genocide. She sought the following: to deny immigration to the "feebleminded"; to impose a rigid policy of sterilization and segregation on "dysgenic groups." Some of her goals were identical to those associated with Nazi Germany. Sanger, in fact, criticized philanthrophy wasted on helping those she called "slum mothers" who, in her eyes, were "breeding, and...perpetuating constantly increasing numbers of defectives, delinquents and dependents."

Sanger, most likely, would have hailed the course taken by the Soviet Union where 90 percent of all first pregnancies end in abortion, and the total number of abortions surpassses eight million annually.

Her prejudices against the unborn and certain races was apparent when she said, "The most merciful thing that a large family can do to one of its infant members is to kill it," and "No one can doubt that there are times when an abortion is justifiable, especially in the case of Wops, Dagos, Jews, Spics, and Negroes."

With Sanger as its inspirational leader, Planned Parenthood has become the primary provider of abortion services around the world. The organization has twenty thousand personnel, eight hundred clinics, two hundred affiliates and fifty metropolitan chapters.

In 1970, then Planned Parenthood president, Dr. Alan

Guttmacher, proposed that special facilities called "abortoriums" be established to meet the future demand for abortions. His proposal was more prophetic than he realized. Nearly 100,000 babies were murdered in Planned Parenthood's clinics in 1985.

Although Planned Parenthood claims to emphasize contraception, in 1976 the organization stated the following as one of its objectives:

> Reaffirming and protecting the legitimacy of induced abortion as a necessary back up to contraceptive failure, and extending safe, dignified services to women who seek them.... To provide leadership in making...abortion and sterilization available and fully accessible to all.

In 1962, to avoid giving birth to a drug-deformed baby, "Miss Sherri," hostess on the "Romper Room" television show, flew to Sweden to have an abortion. Doctors had told her there was a 50 percent chance the baby would be deformed, and she was not willing to risk those odds. At the time she said, "I feel I owe a responsibility to the child, and for its sake I don't feel it morally right to bring a deformed child into the world."

A bill which would have permitted aborting a baby where there was a risk of physical or mental defect was debated in the New York State Assembly in 1969. A polio victim testifed:

> What this bill says is that those who are malformed or abnormal have no reason to be part of our society. If we are prepared to say that life should not come into this world malformed or abnormal, then tomorrow we should be prepared

to say that a life already in this world which becomes malformed or abnormal should not be permitted to live.

The bill was subsequently defeated.

The Supreme Court in *Roe v. Wade*, 1973, held it was a woman's right to terminate an unwanted pregnancy. The landmark case was initiated by a Texas woman who wanted an abortion but could not afford the fare to California which had more liberal laws. Since the Court's finding in 1973, the lives of millions of unborn children have been lost and a moral civil war has erupted. *Roe v. Wade* gave the abortionists the foothold they desired, which has resulted in the devaluation of human life in the "land of the free and the home of the brave."

In 1989, in *Webster v. Reproductive Health Services*, the Supreme Court weakened its Roe decision. The Court ruled to permit states to experiment with laws designed to limit abortion on demand. Immediately states such as Pennsylvania proceeded to enact legislation which requires a twenty-four-hour waiting period before an abortion, outlaws abortions after the twenty-fourth week except to save a mother's life, bans abortions for sex selection, and requires that a spouse be notified prior to an abortion.

The state-by-state battle concerning the fate of the unborn has certainly drawn a clear line between "secular" and "Christian." It has also made it incumbent on politicians to state their position on abortion, for they will no longer be able to skirt the issue. Needless to say, political pollsters are scurrying to discover what Americans are thinking concerning abortion.

Opinion polls are reflective of America's secularization. A sampling of adults by the Gallup Organization found that 53 percent did not agree with the Court's Webster decision allowing states to restrict abortions. And 58 percent did not want to see *Roe v. Wade* overturned.

The Planned Parenthood and NOW forces have paraded celebrities in front of the media to sway public opinion against the anti-abortion movement. Actress Joanne Woodward, for example, signed her name to a letter sent to thousands:

> Very soon, we could see a return to the dark days of the past when abortion was a clandestine and treacherous experience that cost women their health and their lives.... Poll after poll shows that four out of five Americans support legal abortion [this is untrue]. But the anti-choice extremists are trying to force their beliefs on all of us, and I'm afraid they may succeed...unless we act.... American women must not be thrown back to that dangerous and degrading time of illegal abortions, when women were branded as criminals and forced to risk their health and their lives... and thousands die.

Organizations like National Right to Life and Operation Rescue have attempted to bring attention to the pro-life position. Pro-lifers claim the unborn should be entitled to equal protection under the law. Until the modern era, that was the case. Still the law in most states perceives an unborn as a human life in incidents of "fetus abuse." If a baby is delivered with traces of a narcotic in his or her blood, the mother can be charged with a crime. Yet, if that same mother had aborted her addicted baby, she would not be charged. Illogical as it is, a growing number of

Americans are rationalizing an ungodly pro-abortion point of view.

Loudly and vigilantly, the Church has a responsibility to declare God's love for the unborn. But some churches are evidently not convinced God cares, for their denominational leaders have openly advocated full abortion rights. As *Newsweek* reported, this has resulted in a degree of infighting.

> Protestants are quite free to ignore the stands their leaders take on moral issues. In a large and geographically diverse denomination like the United Methodist Church, the abortion issue has become a major source of tension between the local congregations and the church's more liberal national officials.

Due to conflicting opinions within the Church on such issues as abortion and homosexuality, the average person is theologically marooned, left to discover the scriptural position for himself. Events like "Creative Option Day," hosted by California Lutheran University, merely add to the confusion. One class was entitled "Preserving the Right to Safe and Legal Abortion," taught by a key speaker for the California Abortional Rights Action League. "Lesbian Lives" was another class offered. Sadly, these lectures, according to a brochure, were sponsored in cooperation with four local churches. For the unbeliever and non-churchgoer, these inconsistencies lead to mass confusion.

Pro-lifers—including church groups—have begun to learn the importance of using the media, staging protests, and networking with like-minded organizations. But recently pro-abortionists have experienced some success in the courts in their effort to silence pro-life forces. A 1989 court decision gave credence to a racketeering suit brought by NOW against Operation Rescue. The court ruled that anyone blocking pregnant women from entering an abortion clinic may be prosecuted.

"Secularism advances as orthodoxy retreats." Pro-lifers and the Church must not flee confrontation out of fear, passivity, or preoccupation. Otherwise, secularism will thrive unabated.

EUTHANASIA

Dr. Jack Kevorkian has designed a machine that will enable terminally ill patients to kill themselves. It is a suicide machine which uses a drug to induce a heart attack. Critics argue the device could, ultimately, be employed by those who are not terminally ill.

According to Elizabeth Skoglund, author of *Life on the Line*, there is increasing pressure being put on the elderly to commit euthanasia. This is another sign of a Christian nation gone awry.

Dr. Christopher De Giorgio, a neurologist at Los Angeles County USC Medical Center, reported there "are more cases of involuntary euthanasia practiced in the Netherlands than actually voluntary euthanaisa.... The handicapped, the elderly, are afraid to go to hospitals because they're afraid of involuntary euthanasia."

Secularists are attempting to introduce similar practices to America.

In Nazi Germany, euthanasia started with the sick, then the socially unproductive, then those with conflicting ideology. Distressingly, courts in America have opened the door to euthanasia by ruling that people have the constitutional right to death. The Georgia Supreme Court, for instance, gave a thirty-three-year-old quadriplegic the right to shut off the ventilator he relied on to breathe.

Dr. Paul Marx, professor of sociology, said:

> Abortionists and euthanasians constantly accuse those of us who defend innocent life of improperly imposing our religious values on them.... The death peddlers, of course, impose their own secular religion or value system on others, and in the process they impose death as well.... Abortion and euthanasia are not private, sectarian issues but are issues of the broadest public morality, that basic morality which is the foundation of a viable society.[5]

THE ACLU AND RELIGIOUS RIGHTS

The American Civil Liberties Union (ACLU) boasts that it exists to protect the rights of the individual. The ACLU, however, has seldom aspired to protect the religious liberties of mainline Christians.

In William A. Donohue's book, *The Politics of the American Civil Liberties Union,* he said:

> From the Union's perspective, separation between church and state means erecting an iron curtain between the two institutions. It is skeptical, if not distrustful, of the ambitions of the clergy. Freedom is won by relegating religion to a purely private sphere remote from the body politic. In fact, the establishment of a free society is predicated on the idea that religion must be surgically removed from culture. Freedom to worship must be protected but a free people will guard against

the untoward consequences that religious influence might bring. Therefore, a cultural vivi-section is in order: remove religion and immunize society (via the legislature and judiciary) against its reoccurrence.[6]

The ACLU's bias against religious rights is well-documented, said Donohue:

Even when the ACLU was formed, it did not mention freedom of religion as one of its objectives, although it did include all the other components of the First Amendment as well as a commitment to racial equality. That the ACLU ignored freedom of religion was no oversight: the politically driven liberal organization, dedicated to labor and in opposition to capitalism, had no reason to make religious freedom one of its objectives.[7]

Beginning with the Scopes Trial, the ACLU has fought creationism being taught in the classroom, school prayer and Bible reading, church tax exemptions, blue laws, "In God We Trust" on our coins, the Pledge of Allegiance, sacred holidays, Nativity scenes and more.

George Will accurately summed up the ACLU's attitude and activities when he said:

These people want to use state power to purge the social milieu of certain things offensive, but not at all harmful, to them. There is a meanness, even bullying, in this—a disagreeable delight in using the community's law divisively, to abolish traditions enjoyed by neighbors.[8]

NINE

SOCIAL ISSUES: "A SEA OF RELATIVITY"

The only thing necessary for the triumph of evil is
for good men to do nothing.
— Edmund Burke

Every culture must cope with a unique set of social
problems. How a society responds to these crises is often
an accurate barometer of its commitment to God and
scriptural principles. When one studies America's treatment of such social dilemmas as the increasing crime rate,
the absence of patriotism, and the spread of AIDS, one
conclusion is inevitable: this nation no longer seeks Divine wisdom, nor does it base its decisions on the Word
of God. Without God's guidance and a biblical foundation to undergird society, social problems persist and
secularism advances.

173

BILLY THE KID TO BOESKY

Beginning with Cain and Abel, crime has been a part of man's existence. Since the inception of this nation, criminals have been frowned upon by Americans. When apprehended, lawbreakers were incarcerated for lengthy terms and many were sentenced to death. Men like Billy the Kid and Al Capone were feared and despised by the public and viewed as a threat to public safety. In recent years, however, Americans have developed a peculiar fascination and tolerance for villains of the past. They have become folk-heroes to a generation of youthful minds and inspirations to a growing criminal element.

During the days of the Wild West, gunslingers and scarf-faced outlaws roamed the countryside. Marshals, bounty hunters, and an occasional posse of townspeople saddled their horses in hopes of bringing desperados to justice. Most believed criminal acts deserved to be punished. And lawmen and common citizens were bent on doing whatever was necessary to ensure that their town was not overrun and their local bank pilfered.

During the bootlegging days of mobster Al Capone, public sentiment mounted against him and other underworld crime figures. Though citizens did not become personally involved in the struggle to bring "Scarface" and his contemporaries to justice, there was intense pressure placed on law enforcement authorities to thwart the thriving empire of organized crime. To the delight of millions, Capone and others were finally convicted and sent to prison. Justice was served.

One obvious indicator of secularism's advancement in modern society is the apparent tolerance of crime and abandonment of a system which places justice in high regard. Today, killers are released into society, high powered attorneys build legal walls of protection around their guilty clients, and the "rehabilitation" of prisoners has become an oddity.

Jesus Christ prescribed the Ten Commandments as the basis for human behavior. Those who violated these laws would face the natural consequences of their wicked deeds. Surely Christ balanced His message of justice with compassion, but not to the extent that He excused or condoned sin. America has drifted from these principles. "Sin" and "crime" have been banished from our vocabulary; men are no longer held responsibile for their actions. In defiance to God's intentions as detailed in Scripture, violators receive more compassion than their victims. But in the sea of relativity of this age, men are given liberties without responsibility. In the interest of the individual, the interest of the whole (society) has been sacrificed.

Due primarily to overcrowding in prison facilities and "forgiving" laws, the judicial system has felt compelled to parole dangerous felons. One well-known case involved actress Theresa Saldana, whose attacker stabbed her with a knife ten times. The man served seven years in prison and was due to be released—even though he had made threats on Saldana's life while behind bars. Only a last minute reprieve kept the man, temporarily, from being discharged.

A lenient parole system is one of the reasons cited for the rise in white-collar crime. Men like Ivan Boesky, the investor who engaged in insider trading on Wall Street, are frequently slapped on the wrist and sent on their way. Boesky's attorneys petitioned the court to allow their client to serve three thousand hours as an unpaid volunteer at a community food bank as part of his punishment. He had already agreed to pay $100 million in civil fines and penalties, but this was an attempt by his counsel to prevent incarceration. Boesky would eventually spend two years in prison, but many white-collar criminals, though apprehended, never serve a sentence.

Gang-related crime is also on the rise as gang members feel less vulnerable to law enforcement authorities and less fearful of a judicial system seemingly bent on finding ways to extricate them. Gang violence in metropolitan areas has transformed city streets into war zones. At night, streets become eerily desolate as families stay indoors, afraid of getting caught in the crossfire. Drug deals are administered in daylight on street corners; and thefts and murders committed by gangs are frequently left unreported and unresolved, thus furthering the perception that "crime pays."

Meanwhile, government officials and sociologists argue over possible solutions to the cesspool of crime and corruption enveloping our inner cities and suburbs. According to Chuck Colson, the crime rate declines with increased religious activity, and vice versa. Our leaders, nevertheless, seek secular solutions to spiritual problems; they ignore the obvious: that we must return to being "one nation under God, indivisible, with liberty and justice for all."

A PATRIOTIC FIRE?

In 1989 the Supreme Court entertained a case which dealt with the right of a U.S. citizen to burn the American flag. The Court, from the outset, debated the two principal issues at hand: the First Amendment right to exercise free speech and patriotism.

The case stemmed from a symbolic protest at the 1984 Republican Convention in Dallas. A small band of protesters were outside the convention hall yelling, "America, the red, white and blue. We spit on you." Snatching a flag hanging outside a bank building, the group proceeded to set it on fire. Gregory Johnson, a member of the Revolutionary Communist Youth Brigade, was fined $2,000 and sentenced to one year in jail for violating the state's flag desecration law.

Eventually the case was heard by the U.S. Supreme Court. After winning a landmark decision, Johnson said, "Liberty and justice for all is a lie. I am not an American; I'm a proletarian internationalist."

At a time when patriotism is wanting, the Court ruled that burning the flag was an acceptable form of political protest. Justice William Brennan wrote for the majority, "The way to preserve the flag's special role is not to punish those who feel differently about these matters. It is to persuade them that they are wrong."

Justice William Rehnquist, in dissent, said it was difficult to imagine that a government would instruct soldiers to "fight and perhaps die for the flag" and yet not punish individuals for "the public burning of the banner under which they fight."

Laws against flag burning have been in place for decades, although, until recently, seldom has anyone been prosecuted for the offense. President George Bush and leaders from the two major parties called for a constitutional amendment which would permit Congress and states "to prohibit the physical desecration of the flag."

More controversy erupted over the flag at Chicago's School of the Art Institute. A student's "artwork" involved the use of the flag as a floormat to wipe one's feet. War veterans angrily demanded that the flag be lifted from the floor and hung with due respect. But liberals maintained it was the student's right to express himself as he wished.

The issue embodied in the fate of the flag is patriotism. In a society where secular humanism reigns, absolutes become obsolete. Traditionally held values such as love of God and country are smothered by the teachings of relativity. And when a society's moral base becomes the victim of secularism, religious beliefs and patriotism are two values which are hastily discarded.

An essay published in *Rolling Stone Magazine* exemplified the shrinking patriotic spirit in this country. Twenty seven percent of the young people surveyed said they could not identify any situation that would prompt them to enlist for military service. Many Americans have taken this nation for granted; they are content to bask in their freedoms without accepting the responsibilities which accompany life in a republic. They take pride in their autonomy but are disrespectful of a flag which represents freedom and a system which is the vehicle for liberty.

AIDS AND POLITICS

The tragedy of the AIDS crisis is that it has become a political tool of those espousing the homosexual agenda. The losers in this tactical war are those suffering with the disease.

Reported AIDS cases continue to increase and yet factions within the homosexual community refuse to submit to measures which could limit the spread of the virus. Therein lies the irony of the AIDS establishment: they place more emphasis on legitimizing the homosexual lifestyle and fighting "discriminatory" actions against AIDS victims than they do fostering a prevention program.

Politicians and health officials—fearful of being criticized by the homosexual establishment—have become
fiscal pawns. Others are accomplices to this debacle by
their mere silence. Meanwhile, millions of tax dollars
have been allotted for AIDS research, while equally dis-
tressing diseases remain unresearched.

Elizabeth Whelan, president of the American Council
on Science and Health, attended the International Conference on AIDS. The meeting opened with an AIDS
manifesto demanding "full legal recognition of lesbian
and gay relationships." She wrote in the *New York Times*:

> I think such recognition is not an essential part of
> an AIDS prevention program.... There is no repre-
> sentation in the AIDS establishment that I can
> discern of the mainstream values and beliefs of
> most Americans.... If the aim of the AIDS estab-
> lishment is truly to save lives and not merely to
> advance a political agenda, then AIDS education
> must be sophisticated and sensitive, and respect a
> diversity of values.

America's response to AIDS—like its response to
crime and flag burning—is reflective of a value system
shifting toward secularism. Courts are afraid to label
crimes as sin; love of God and country is becoming less
fashionable; and the lives of AIDS patients have been
reduced to chess pieces in a game to further an ideology
contrary to the Word of God.

TEN

ECONOMICS: MONEY MAKES AMERICA GO 'ROUND

We must choose either to sink completely into materialism or to pursue a freedom grounded in spiritual values.
—Ronald Berman paraphrasing
Alexander Solzhenitsyn

Materialism. Greed. Consumption. These words have become synonymous with the American version of capitalism, for the vast majority of business decisions in this country are not based on the Judeo-Christian ethic. Morality has been exorcised from the business community as if it were a curse to success. That is not to suggest that, at any given time, business transactions in America were fully governed by biblical principles; but certainly Judeo-Christian values played a more prominent role in years past than they do within the business circles of today.

Adam Smith, in 1776, published his *Wealth of Nations*. According to college professor Robert Heilbroner, Smith's book attempted to formulate the laws of the market: "What he sought was 'the invisible hand,' as he called it, whereby 'the private interests and passions of men' are led in the direction 'which is most agreeable to the interest of the whole society.'" Smith said, "No society can surely be flourishing and happy, of which by far the greater part of the numbers are poor and miserable." Heilbroner wrote that Smith also preached that self-interest must be "held in abeyance" for man "to form a sympathetic notion of the moral merits of a case."

In the second half of the nineteenth century, a growing number of businessmen began to ignore the Judeo-Christian values taught by Smith and others. They chose to "compartmentalize" their faith. In other words, their business dealings were not affected by their biblical convictions. Business practices, so they rationalized, were immune to scriptural influence. "Business is business," they proclaimed. Perhaps it was the massive growth and size of financial transactions which initiated a redefining of "acceptable practices" in the marketplace. On the heels of the industrial revolution business empires were built at meteoric rates; and, just as quickly, fortunes were lost. The fight for survival and success motivated many business tycoons to compromise their traditional beliefs. The pursuit of the dollar justified whatever underhanded tactics were determined necessary. And, as a result, the dollar became the master of many.

Economic concerns and the sweeping lust for money have, unquestionably, had their effect on this nation's commitment to the Almighty. "No man can serve two masters."

RAILROAD TYCOONS

In 1869, the first transcontinental railroad was completed. The effect of this transportation facility on the expansion of businesses to the West was monumental. The fortunes it amassed were staggering. With vast amounts of cash seemingly to be made, the struggle to control railroad routes intensified. Banks were bombarded with requests for capital. Men like Jay Gould and Collis Huntington borrowed thousands of dollars to expand their rail lines. Financial disaster eventually befell many of these speculators, but the age of big and bigger business had been born. Rate wars, monopolies, price fixing, and businessmen with extreme economic and political clout characterized the 1880s and beyond.

J.P. Morgan, a prominent financier of the railroad industry, epitomized the power of the moguls of this era. They did far more than set the standards for business and dictate financial and social trends. During a crisis in the U.S. Treasury in 1895, for example, President Grover Cleveland called on Morgan for help. The government's gold reserves were less than $10,000; default appeared inevitable. Morgan in turn orchestrated a private bond sale to bail out the government.

The mores and practices publicly advanced by revered financial giants like Morgan were not always consistent with Christendom. Stanley Jackson, author of a J.P. Morgan biography, said, "He considered himself a good Christian but was guilty of all but one of the seven deadly sins [he was not slothful]. He was an affectionate family man but also a notorious womanizer."

Morgan's son, Pierpont, was the heir apparent to the family fortune. On the surface, Pierpont appeared to have more affection for Christianity. He had breakfast with his minister each week, contributed large amounts of money to the church, and attended services regularly. Even so, said Jackson, "he attempted to dominate everyone who opposed him from the president of the United States to the trade union leaders pressing for more humane conditions...." And like his father, he too maintained a double moral standard.

ROCKEFELLER AND FORD

When John D. Rockefeller made a $100,000 donation to the Congregationalist Board of Foreign Missions, one minister rushed to the podium to demand that the "tainted money" be rejected. The minister said:

Is this clean money? Can any man, can any institution, knowing its origins, touch it without being defiled? [It has been accumulated] by methods as heartless, as cynically iniquitous as any that were employed by the Roman plunderers or robber barons of the Dark Ages. In the cool brutality with which properties are wrecked, securities destroyed, and people by the hundreds robbed of their little, all to build up the fortunes of the multimillionaires, we have an appalling revelation of the kind of monster that a human being may become.[1]

Rockefeller was considered by some as an unrepentant "white-collar" criminal who had wielded unfair influence over the lives of others. The financial czar, meanwhile, maintained he was a Christian who had been misinterpreted and unfairly maligned. It was this notion that he had been mistreated in the press which provoked him to expand his philanthropy. Besides distributing dimes to common folk, he gave thousands of dollars to religious organizations.

Though despised for his economic prowess, Rockefeller viewed his ability to make money as a gift from God—a gift which he had a responsibility to nurture. His critics, however, questioned his tactics for making money, claiming God would not condone his manner of conducting business. Regardless, to the modern generation, John D. Rockefeller has become the embodiment of capitalism, success, and economic supremacy.

A contemporary of Rockefeller's, Henry Ford, also left his mark on future generations of corporate executives. Ford's automobile manufacturing exploits changed forever America's method of doing business. Frederich Allen, in his book *The Big Change*, said, "Ford was ruining the labor market, he was putting crazy ideas into workmen's heads, he would embarrass companies which couldn't possibly distribute such largess, he was a crude self-advertiser." He was also a "merciless competitor."

Ford helped bring to fruition an economic revolt in the early 1920s. Reported Allen:

> [The] change in the status of the automobile from a luxury for the few to a necessity for the many [was] a change which...progressively transformed American communities and daily living habits and ideas throughout the half century.... In 1915 there were less than 2 1/2 million cars registered

in the United States. By 1920 there were over 9 million; by 1925, nearly 20 million; by 1930, over 26 1/2 million.[2]

Men like Ford and Rockefeller were power-brokers during an era which was formative to modern capitalism and American society as a whole. They were the predecessors of modern day billionaires like Donald Trump and Ted Turner—public men who thrive on their ability to make lucrative, highly visible business deals. These are the modern day idols of businessmen and women who have set their sights on profit, acquisition and status... with little regard for social casualties.

INDUSTRIALIZATION AND THE DEPRESSION

The level of spiritual fervency in America has paralleled, to a certain extent, the economic condition of the nation. More specifically, the financial status of the common citizen has had an effect on the spiritual awareness of the individual.

Prior to the period of industrial expansion—at the turn of the twentieth century—families were content to work at home, forgo luxury, to persevere in economic hardship. The pace of life allowed for spiritual reflection, Bible reading, and prayer. But the "American conscience" changed with the technological advances of the industrial revolution. People wanted to experience new inventions: automobiles, farm equipment, and factory machinery. Thus, a new lifestyle and pace evolved from the pursuit and acquisition of new technologies. Time once set aside for spiritual activities was consumed by other interests, obligations, and longer work days brought on by industrialization.

Perhaps the greatest transformation ushered in by the industrial period was an unhealthy enchantment with material objects. Acquiring material possessions became an obsession for many.

Literature, including some theological publications, began justifying the quest for prosperity. In the 1920s, for example, in *The Man Nobody Knows*, author Bruce Barton "set himself the task of proving that Jesus was not merely 'the founder of modern business,'" said Loren Baritz, "but that His principles would be effective in the twentieth as in the first century. A true understanding of Jesus' business acumen would result in hard cash and personal power for his latest disciples in American business and industry. Christian discipleship, according to Barton, was in fact the surest way to a healthy profit and loss statement. The obvious vulgarity of Barton's argument should not obscure the fact of its enormous contemporary popularity (it was a best seller), if not actual influence."

Profit, massive profits, became the brass ring of spawning businesses. To increase the take, flawed products were distributed to the public and business owners began hiring children, aliens, and women at meager wages to work in "sweat shops." Ethics were sacrificed in the name of reaping financial reward.

A vast majority of Americans during the early 1900s were satisfied with their lot in life. Business was booming and America was becoming self-sufficient. Dependence on Divine provision and spiritual awareness, however, began to waver. "Success" had left its stain on Christianity as well. "From 1880 on the wealth of the American people increased greatly. This had an effect on the life of the churches.... With the new industrial age churches began to place great emphasis on business efficiency.

187

Successful businessmen were given places on the financial boards of churches" (B.K. Kuiper, *The Church in History*). This new emphasis and influx of business people served to secularize the message and the mission of the Church. Rather than lead, church officials began to conform their views to those of their congregations. A wave of accommodation swept through mainline denominations.

With the stock market crash in October, 1929, Americans' hopes for prosperity and affluence crumbled. The nation's economy was at a standstill. Befuddled economic philosophers, government officials, and businessmen threw up their hands as enthusiasm for capitalism reached all time lows. Frederick Allen said:

> Not only had the big bankers of 1929 failed to stop the panic, but as time went on the inability of financiers generally to cope with the down trend, their loss of confidence in their own economic convictions, and the downfall of the banking system itself all advertised their helplessness.... The depression sharply lowered the prestige of businessmen.[3]

The U.S. government finally intervened to restore a semblance of stability. Consequently, government became the answer to man's material pangs in a period when business and technology had purportedly failed.

The effects of the Great Depression, 1929-1941, were numerous, said Caroline Bird, author of *The Invisible Scar*:

> The Depression expanded the role of government, and of Federal government at the expense of states. It stimulated business to social con-

science and professionalized corporate management. It changed the balance of power in family life in favor of women while discouraging marriage and motherhood. It held back and isolated Negroes, Jews, and women by making it easy to discriminate against them in employment, and it converted the public school from stepping-stone to refuge for the unemployed. It turned intellectuals to the left, slowed the application of technology, kept most of the nation ill-housed, and prevented the natural spread of population to suburbs. It influenced fashions in women's clothing, amusements, architecture, lovemaking, and child rearing.[4]

The Church was not spared the influences of the Depression as rescue mission-like churches arose in metropolitan areas, amidst cries for help from the throngs of unemployed. Many churches began to espouse a social gospel as meeting the tangible needs of the less-fortunate supplanted meeting their spiritual needs.

Some churches suffered losses in their membership due to their lack of support for the growing labor movement. Blue-collar workers believed church leaders were withholding their support for labor unions because the churches were receiving money from big business. As a result, churches were perceived as lacking sympathy for blue-collar workers and the common man who was living at the poverty level.

America, historians contend, did not climb from its economic disaster until the 1941 bombing of Pearl Harbor. Even so, Roosevelt was credited with lifting Americans from their knees and restoring their financial dignity by manufacturing jobs. Many began to look to government for sustenance rather than the Creator; this in itself served to desensitize people to the local church.

BABY BOOMERS

Following World War II America experienced unprecedented economic expansion. Materialism once again reared its ugly head. Two cars, a two-story house, two kids, and a television set became the obsession. Church membership, however, fit neatly into the American dream of peace, prosperity, and material preoccupation. But church attendance, on the other hand, did not fit into their bag of aspirations. Parents, lacking a commitment to the church but realizing the importance of a religious environment and religious tradition, began sending their children to Sunday School. The fact remains that for many adults earthly possessions were their god. The hippy generation of the '60s was, in part, fueled by a philosophical rebellion against this "possession obsession."

The materialistic inclinations of the Post World War II generation were fostered by some church leaders, business executives, and the writings of men like Napoleon Hill. His best-selling book *Think and Grow Rich* was the Bible for many aspiring capitalists:

All down the ages, the religionists have admonished struggling humanity to 'have faith' in this, that, and other dogma or creed, but they have failed to tell people how to have faith. They have not stated that 'faith is a state of mind, and that it may be induced by self suggestion....' Faith is the starting point of all accumulation of riches.... If you wish evidence of the power of faith, study the achievements of men and women who have employed it. At the head of the list comes the Nazarene....[5]

In the 1990s Hill's philosophy still has its followers, though it flourishes under other names: positive thinking, New Age, and more. The prosperity doctrine—a secular ideology—has infiltrated the Church, so much so, that Christians have reinterpreted Scripture to justify their materialistic approach to life. In doing so, they have polluted Christ's message, which can have no other effect than to proliferate the secularization of the nation.

ELEVEN

GLOBAL CONFLICT: THE SPOILS OF WAR

We have our last chance. If we do not now devise some greater and more equitable system, Armageddon will be at our door. The problem is basically theological and involves a spiritual recrudescence and improvement of human character. It must be of the spirit if we are to save the flesh.
        —General Douglas MacArthur
        signing of Japanese surrender,
        end of World War II

Global military conflict, throughout the ages, has had an effect on the pysche and spiritual tone of nations. Since the beginning of man, war has left its hideous inscription on societies. The scars of battle have not been limited to physical wounds, however, for the emotional and spiritual bruises have sometimes been deep, enduring, and undistinguishable.

War has changed the attitudes, beliefs, and lifestyles

of entire nations; it has also united countries in service to God but, more frequently, it has shattered a people spiritually. Anything which alters the emotional balance of a mass of people to that extent will invariably have an effect on the nation's spiritual consciousness and the Church.

REVOLUTIONARY WAR

To many American patriots the Revolutionary War was a religious battle. "With few exceptions, the clergy... gave their hearty support to the war.... Many made resistance and independence a holy cause. Many joined the army as officers or chaplains" (B.K. Kuiper, *The Church in History*). Some churches sided with England, but for the most part, ministers and congregations were supportive of the Revolution—a war which to them had spiritual consequences.

Because of General George Washington's leadership and his strong commitment to Judeo-Christian principles, said *A Country Made by War* author Geoffrey Perret, "There was no other army in the eighteenth century like it: religious, inoculated, and forbidden gambling.... The sobriety and modesty, the interest in character and morals that Washington's army brought to warfare helped create the American military tradition and augured a new style."

THE CIVIL WAR

The dispute over slavery mushroomed into civil war, but the issue proved divisive long before one bullet was fired. Theological schisms over human rights resulted in church splits and congregational infighting. Churches located in both Union and Confederate states were equally bunkered in their beliefs, declaring biblical justification for their position. The Baptist Missionary Society discontinued its relationship with the Baptists of the North. The Methodists, Presbyterians, and Episcopalians experienced similar severings.

The theological uproar cast a shadow over the Church and the nation. President Lincoln attempted to reunite the country through a spiritual revival, or at least a renewed emphasis on the need for spiritual guidance. He set aside days of national fasting and prayer and days of thanksgiving. But it would be decades before the nation's spiritual scars would heal and the repercussions would fade. During this era many religious institutions suffered tragic losses: influence, respect, and potential converts.

TWO WORLD WARS

Frederick Allen wrote:

The war (World War I) had pulled millions of young men and women out of their accustomed environments, and given them a taste of freedom.... With many of these young people the postwar reaction took a special form: it was easy for them to think of themselves as a generation who had been condemned to go through the hell of war because of the mistakes of their elders, whose admonitions on any subject must therefore be suspect. At any rate, by 1920 the rebellion against puritanism and stuffiness was widely visible, and it gained in impetus as the decade progressed.[1]

This changing attitude and consensus was precipitated by a changing Church. B.K. Kuiper said, "The years of World War I and those immediately following were boom years in the United States.... While the church service was...made more elaborate, church attendance was declining, for in many cases the preaching of God's Word was disappearing."

Meanwhile, the secular writings of F. Scott Fitzgerald, Ernest Hemmingway, and other secular humanists were being widely read. Ungodly philosophies encroached on territory previously monopolized by the Church: the minds of the young.

Philosopher Friedrich Nietzsche's theory that God had become irrelevant began to gain acceptance, perhaps because of the Church's impotency and the growing skepticism of a God who would allow the gross horrors of war to occur. Nietzsche maintained that the existence of God was a moot issue because man lived as though God was dead. He said, "What is more dangerous to the human race than any crime? ...Christianity!.... I condemn Christianity."

Chuck Colson said of Nietzsche's theory:

> The effect...can be seen in the despair that followed World War I, in the void that gave rise to fascism, in the militant atheism that has claimed countless lives in Russia and China.... 'The devaluation of all values' is what the death of God has meant to politics. Distinctions between right and wrong, justice and injustice have become meaningless. No objective guide is left to choose between 'all men are created equal' and the 'weak to the wall.'[2]

A case has been made that Nietzsche—a German

scholar—provided a theological license for world domination which led to both world wars. Paul Johnson, in his book *Modern Times*, wrote:

> Nietzsche...saw God not as an invention but as a casualty, and his demise as in some important sense an historical event, which would have dramatic consequences. He wrote in 1886: 'The greatest event of recent times—that God is dead, that the belief in the Christian God is no longer tenable—is beginning to cast its first shadows over Europe.' Among the advanced races, the decline and ultimately the collapse of the religious impulse would leave a huge vacuum.... Nietzsche rightly perceived that the most likely candidate [to fill the vacuum] would be what he called the 'will to power....' In place of religious belief, there would be secular ideology.... And, above all, the 'will to power' would produce a new kind of messiah, uninhibited by any religious sanctions whatever, and with an unappeasable appetite for controlling mankind. The end of the old order, with an unguided world adrift in a relativistic universe, was a summons to such gangster-statesmen to emerge. They were not slow to make their appearance.[3]

In William Jennings Bryan's unused closing statement for the Scopes Trial he referred to Englishman Benjamin Kidd's book *The Science of Power*. Kidd claimed that Darwinism—that "the evolution of the world" was "the product of natural selection in never-ceasing war" and "a purely mechanical and material process resting on force"—was interpreted by Nietzsche and "delivered with the fury and intensity of genius." Bryan added, "Kidd says that Nietzsche gave Germany the doctrine of Darwin's efficient animal in the voice of his superman, and that Bernhardi and the military textbooks in due time gave Germany the doctrine of the superman translated into the national policy of the super-state aiming at world power." In Robert W. Cherny's book *A Righteous Cause*, he said:

> Another factor in Bryan's increasing antagonism toward evolution derived from his conviction that it had laid 'the foundation for the bloodiest war in history.' Evolution, he thought, had produced Friedrich Nietzsche's writings, in which Bryan discerned 'a defense, made in advance, of all the atrocities practiced by militarists of Germany.'

The secular faith of British Prime Minister Neville Chamberlain and other world leaders, some have suggested, precipitated the Second World War. Chamberlain was a Unitarian who, contrary to Scripture, believed that man was basically good. Because of this theological conviction, historians have declared that he and other leaders naively trusted Hitler—the "messiah" Nietzsche predicted.

Chamberlain said in 1937:

> For any government to deny to their people what must be their plainest and simplest right [to live in peace and happiness without the nightmare of war] would be to betray their trust and to call down upon their heads the condemnation of all mankind.... I do not believe that such a govern-

ment anywhere exists among civilized peoples. I am convinced that the aim of every statesman worthy of the name, to whatever country he belongs, must be happiness of the people for whom and to whom he is responsible, and in that faith I am sure that a way can and will be found to free the world from the curse of armaments and the fears that give rise to them, and to open up a happier, and a wiser future for mankind.

Once the attrocities of Nazi Germany were unfolded to the world, Chamberlain's optimism—born out of Secular Humanism—would be dispelled as ignorance.

The United States finally, reluctantly, entered World War II. Perret reported:

The war had come to a country riddled with class tensions, class anger. Since the end of the frontier the gap between the top one-fifth and the bottom one fifth had been widening. For the only time in this century that gap narrowed as well-paid jobs became available to all willing to work.... As the war drew everyone into a historic shared experience it alleviated the American condition—loneliness. This heritage—from beginnings in vast spaces; reborn in the towering, impersonal cities of concrete and steel; sharpened by the misery of the depression—was a psychological burden that drove millions to psychoanalysis or drink, knowing neither one was the true answer. The healing effects of the war on the nation's psyche, making a nation of individuals feel for a time as one, was a profound and priceless experience, easily as important as the material results.[4]

The War brought Americans together temporarily, but, with the absence of a Christian consensus or spiritual basis for battle, the so-called "unity" and "healing" were short-lived. In reality, the wounds of war were hidden, and a new set of secular values partly forged by the conflict were yet to be unveiled. In the end, few could say war was a friend.

Wrote Allen:

> During World War I there had been a live crusading spirit—and there had also been considerable opposition to the war. This time (World War II) there was no opposition. During the whole three years and eight months that the United States fought, there was no anti-war faction, no organized pacifist element, no objection to huge appropriations, no noticeable opposition to the draft.[5]

Catholic novelist George Bernanos added:

> Questions of justice, prudence, responsibility and consequences were set aside in pursuit of a technique to win the war. Though the bomb hastened the end of the war, it would shape civilization's values for the remainder of the century. Just as technique had triumphed over reason, so expediency would triumph over morality.[6]

The widespread support for the war and pressure to win at any cost created problems for the Church, according to the Reverend Henry Fosdick. He wrote:

> Beyond helping individuals I was deeply concerned in my preaching with a second purpose: to

keep the church Christian despite the unchristian nature of war. Arguments about a 'just war' have for centuries beguiled Christians into baptizing bloody slaughter in the name of Christ. In the present evil estate of the world bloody slaughter may sometimes be unavoidable, but it is blasphemy to degrade Christ into giving it his benediction though it represents His will and way of life. In World World II, for example, one preacher argued that because God sends men to hell... therefore Christians may use violence in war.[7]

Nevertheless, as in the days of the Revolutionary War, many Americans—especially Christians—perceived World War II as a "holy" conflict ordained by God to conquer evil.

LIGHTS, CAMERA, WAR

Soviet Premier Nikita Khrushchev, in the late 1950s, said, "Captialism is a worn out old mare while socialism is new, young, and full of teeming energy.... We will bury capitalism.... Socialism will inevitably succeed capitalism.... The rotten [capitalist] world is collapsing. Friends, let's drink, let's laugh, let's rejoice."

Many Americans feared the Soviet leader's statements were prophetic as the 1960s unraveled: assassinations, riots, and the Vietnam War—a war which was piped into the living room of every U.S. citizen.

The failure to win the longlasting war in Vietnam, together with the nightly television footage, caused further distress among the American people. Unlike previous wars, Americans could not escape the bloody images of the battlefield. They were mandatory participants, therby provoking the public to vent its frustrations through protest and other means.

Perret said:

> The way in which three presidents pursued the war in Vietnam not only guaranteed failure but made the ruination of the U.S. Army as certain as tomorrow's sunrise. The damage spread, like a pandemic, around the globe. There were riots, breakdowns of discipline, even fragging at bases in the United States and Western Europe. Fighting ability crumbled as combat units worldwide were stripped of vital equipment, weapons, ammunition stocks and trained personnel to feed the war in Southeast Asia.[8]

Alexander Solzhenitsyn commented:

> The most cruel mistake occurred with the failure to understand the Vietnam War. Some people sincerely wanted all wars to stop just as soon as possible; others believed that the way should be left open for national, or Communist, self-determination in Vietnam. But in fact, members of the U.S. antiwar movement became accomplices in the betrayal of Far Eastern nations, in the genocide and the suffering today imposed on thirty million people there. Do these convinced pacifists now hear the moans coming from there? Do they understand their responsibility today? Or do they prefer not to hear?[9]

The memory of blood-stained soldiers, tear-stained Vietnamese children, and the shame stemming from the

war still linger. Some Americans feel guilty for abandon-
ing the Vietnamese people; others feel guilty for sending
our soldiers to fight in Southeast Asia. Regardless of one's
political persuasions, universally, the Vietnam War evokes
feelings of uneasiness. This is not difficult to understand
when one considers the bombings of innocent villages,
the agent orange scandal, and the gunning down of
several hundred civilians in the South Vietnamese village
of My Lai.

Jonathan Schell, in his book *Observing the Nixon Years*,
wrote:

> Although it may be that the My Lai massacre is an
> isolated incident, in the sense that no other report
> of mass killing of civilians by troops on the ground
> has been brought to light, there can be no doubt
> that such an atrocity was possible only because a
> number of other methods of killing civilians and
> destroying their villages had come to be the rule,
> and not the exception, in our conduct of war.

The Vietnam War gave the sixties movement at home
a much needed cause. Radical marchers rallied against
the war, but their verbal and non-verbal message spread
to include a denunciation of traditional values as well.
Some protesters exploited society's guilt to further their
own cause: liberalism.

Peter Collier and David Horowitz wrote in their book
Destructive Generation:

> The manufacture of innocence out of guilt: is
> the eternal work of the Left. The true genius of
> radicalism is constant self-recreation and reap-
> pearance in new guises. Never mind that the

sloughed-off skins it leaves behind are fossilized remains of the death and destruction caused by its past commitments. For Leftists, there are only tomorrows. They never talk about the evil they have done, except superficially, to imply...that it has increased their moral sensitivity. But they are always anxious to discuss the utopia to come.... How does the Left maintain its belief against the crushing weight of its failures in the past? By recycling its innocence, which allows it to be born again in its utopian faith. The utopianism of the Left is a secular religion...its promise an earthly kingdom of heaven.

The New Left saw itself as a movement that would design its own American future, without imitating foreign models—a sort of American studies project of the real world. The phrase 'participatory democracy' captured the intention to make the promise of America real. Its first campaign—for civil rights—was based on a belief in this promise. The Vietnam War provided an opportunity for this optimism to ferment and then to sour. The speed with which the New Left became disaffected from the nation and from its own early ideals, and the fact that this happened with so little resistance, suggests that the movement had a split personality from the beginning— one part believing in an American radicalism and the other not believing in anything at all.

The sixties are still with us, therefore, as a nostalgic artifact that measures our more somber world and finds it wanting, and also as a goad to radical revival. It has become the decade that would not die, the decade whose long half-life continues to contaminate our own.

Among the byproducts of the Vietnam experience were a rebirth of isolationalism and passivism. Just as significant was the rise in cynicism—which is reflective of a nation without hope in an omnipotent, omnipresent God. A survey conducted by the Media General Associated Press illustrated this; it found that 49 percent of Americans believe World War III will occur and more than 50 percent said it would escalate to all-out nuclear war and end in mass genocide.

TWELVE

THE CHURCH: SECULARISM IN THE SANCTUARY

The two great dangers which threaten the existence of religion are schism and indifference.
    —Alexis de Tocqueville

Pundits and preachers alike have made their living
casting aspersions on the Church. "Christians are to
blame for the moral chaos in America—the decline in
religious conviction," they claim. Though individual
believers and the Church as an institution must assume
responsibility for their apathy which resulted in the
subsequent conquests of secularism, nothing is to be
gained by pointing fingers of condemnation. Thus, this
chapter focuses its attention on the Church's errors of the
past and present soley in the hope that these pitfalls will
be avoided in the future, that the Church will learn from

its mistakes and choose a course of biblical obedience.

Christians, obedient and led by the Spirit, are the antidote for the spiritual poison spreading across the nation. Believers must, therefore, acknowledge their shortcomings and failures, seek God's forgiveness and guidance, and display a renewed desire to serve as God's agents in the civic arena.

THE GREAT RE-AWAKENING

When the Colonialists settled in America, their lives were based on Judeo-Christian principles. The local church was revered, the minister respected, and the tenets of faith held holy. Confirming the religiosity of that era, historian Robert Baird wrote in 1856: "The religion of the overwhelming majority, and which may therefore be called national, is, in all essential points, what was taught by the great Protestant Reformers of the sixteenth century."

But in the eighteenth century, deism and rationalism spread from Europe to American communities and infiltrated the Church. Beliefs once considered sacred were abandoned by many. And as the number of theological dissenters mounted, the once strong Judeo-Christian consensus began to shift ever so slightly. In time, the change became more apparent, for the Church itself had undergone a theological reconstruction. The inerrancy of Scripture, the deity of Jesus Christ, and the existence of Heaven and Hell were among the traditional teachings being disputed from pulpits and within congregations.

Ministers like George Whitefield refused to allow secularism to devour the traditional Church. They set out to reaffirm the truth of the gospel by traveling throughout the colonies, holding one revival meeting after another.

Huge audiences gathered to hear these men proclaim the Word of God, and thousands rededicated their lives to Christ. The Great Awakening was born.

Yale professor Sydney Ahlstrom wrote:

> Between the Glorious Revolution and the War for Independence comes that great spiritual and institutional earthquake, the Evangelical Awakening, a vast and diversifeid religious revival— heralded by Solomon Stoddard's Northampton 'harvests' at the century's turn, continued in the Middle colonies, given classic symbolization by the 'Surprising Conversions' which Jonathan Edwards described in 1735, and gaining colony-wide force throughout the campaigns of George Whitefield during the 1740s, and then rumbling on in many places, especially in the Southern back country down to and through the Revolutionary War. Everywhere the revivals challenged the standing order and disrupted churches; in retropect it can be seen as a massive and enduring intensification of the Puritan impulse as well as a broad nationalization of the American self-consciousness. Among its most important effects were the solidarity it gave to the heretofore divided evangelical community and the sense of providential destiny, which in due time would infect rationalists and enthusiasts alike.[1]

Baird said the Great Awakening "infused a new life into the churches" and that at no time in the history of Christendom was there such a widespread knowledge of the Bible and practical application of its teachings.

Unfortunately the period of revival was cut short by

an outbreak of denominational infighting, which in the end, resulted in church splits and the expansion of liberal and cultic sects. B.K. Kuiper said:

> As the revival faded away certain disagreements arose. The Congregational ministers in New England and the Reformed ministers in New York were divided as to its value. Some favored it, others were against it. The Presbyterian Church was split over the question though later reunited. The Great Awakening also brought about the development of the New England theology, which in the end led to a great weakening of historic Calvinism among the Congregationalists, the Reformed, and the Presbyterians. At the same time a liberal tendency began to show itself, especially in the churches of Boston and vicinity, which in the early nineteenth century resulted in the formation of Unitarian churches.[2]

The American Revolution served to reunite Christians behind the common cause of freedom. Minor theological differences were temporarily set aside for the purpose of putting an end to British oppression. But following the war for independence, the philosophies which had fueled the French Revolution gained new levels of acceptance in America. The effects of Unitarianism, Deism, and Relativism were, unquestionably, an erosion of morality and respect for traditional faiths.

The resurgence of liberal ideology, which had enveloped numerous traditional New England churches, and the outbreak of blatant immorality provoked many evangelicals to action. In the late 1700s a Second Great Awakening began to stir. Revival was spawned on college campuses, missionary societies and seminaries were founded, and Sunday Schools were established. Church attendance increased as reverence for the scriptural way of life became fashionable again.

THE CHURCH AND THE KKK

As the country entered the mid-1800s, it was confronted with an issue which would not only divide the nation but churches as well. As the debate over slavery raged, individual congregations, for the most part, held together while denominations as a whole were severed. Each faction staked a biblical claim to its position on slavery. This theological corruption by many of the churches in the South led to confusion and a distrust of religious authority.

The abominable activities of a "religiously motivated" Ku Klux Klan surely heightened the confusion and emotional furor. Perhaps partly due to the organization's self-alignment with Protestantism, the Klan's membership increased steadily before, during, and after the Civil War.

Hiram Wesley Evans, a Texas dentist, became the imperial wizard of the Klan in 1922. In one of his speeches he typified how the organization, from its inception, twisted Scripture to justify its ungodly ideals:

> We believe the hand of God was in the creation of the American stock and nation. We believe, too, in the right and duty of every man to fight for himself, his own children, his own nation and race. We believe in the parable of the talents, and mean to keep and use those entrusted to us—the race, spirit and nationhood of America.... We

know we are right in the same sense that a good
Christian knows that he has been saved and that
Christ lives.... Protestantism contains more than
religion. It is the expression in religion of the same
spirit of independence, self-reliance and freedom
which are the highest achievements of the Nordic
race.... It has been a distinctly Nordic religion, and
it has been through this religion that the Nordics
have found strength to take leadership of all whites
and the supremacy of the earth. Its destruction is
the deepest purpose of all other peoples, as that
would mean the end of Nordic rule.... The Negro,
the Klan considers a special duty and problem of
the white Americans.... The future of the Klan we
believe in, though it is still in the hands of God and
of our own abilities and consecration and individuals and as a race.

The Klan's hatred-propaganda, camouflaged by religious jargon and slanted Protestant theology, created a
public relations dilemma for the Church. Denominations
seemingly harboring Klan members in their congregations were branded as hypocritical and unsympathetic to
human rights. Some even questioned the justice and
power of a Christian God who would allow these villains
to spread hatred in His name.

THE SOCIAL GOSPEL

At the end of the nineteenth century, the Church turned
to the social gospel to repair its tarnished reputation and
stir Christians from their pews. The Church had become
fixed on ritual, comfort, and denominationalism while
seemingly ignoring the plight of the common man. The

message of the social gospel was, in essence, "please God by working to put an end to social problems, by improving the lives of the less fortunate."

Walter Rauschenbusch is recognized as the father of social Christianity in the United States. While pastoring a small Baptist church in New York City, Rauschenbusch became familiar with the plight of the hungry and hurting. After becoming Professor of Church History at Rochester Theological Seminary in the early 1900s, the reverend published his treatises dealing with the Church's obligation to help the needy citizens of American society. He wrote:

> Social Christianity is adding to the variety of religious experience, and is creating a new type of Christian man who bears a striking family likeness to Jesus of Galilee. The new religious emotions ought to find conscious and social expression. But the Church, which has brought down so rich an equipment from the past for the culture of individual religion, is poverty-stricken in the face of this new need.... The Lord's Prayer is the great prayer of social Christianity. It is charged with what we call 'social consciousness.' It assumes the social solidarity of men as a matter of course. It recognizes the social basis of all moral and religious life even in the most intimate personal relations to God.... Its dominating thought is the moral and religious transformation of mankind in all its social relations. It was left us by Jesus, the great initiator of the Christian revolution; and it is the rightful property of those who follow his banner in the conquest of the world.

John F. Piper, Jr. summarized the reason for the social gospel's rapid growth in his book *The American Churches in World War I*:

> Churchmen in general and Protestants in particular related their practical efforts to their theological understanding of the Kingdom of God. Many of them shared Walter Rauschenbusch's two-fold version of the Kingdom: 'the kingdom of God is divine in its origin, progress and consummation' and 'the kingdom is for each of us the supreme task and supreme gift of God. By accepting it as a task, we experience it as a gift. By laboring for it we enter into the joy and peace of the kingdom as our divine fatherland and habitation.'

In his book *Christianity and Social Crisis*, published in 1914, Rauschenbusch wrote:

> We have seen that their [Jesus and His twelve disciples] religious concern was not restricted to private religion and morality, but dealt preeminently with the social and political life of their nation. Would they limit its range today?... Christian morality finds its highest dignity and its constant corrective in making the kingdom of God the supreme aim to which all minor aims must contribute and from which they gain their moral quality. The church substituted itself for the kingdom of God, and thereby put the advancement of a tangible and very human organization in the place of the moral uplifting of humanity. By that substitution the ethical plane of all actions was subtly and terribly lowered.... What is

connected with the churches is religious; what is apart from them is supposed to be secular.... Efforts to fight tuberculosis or secure parks and playgrounds are viewed as secular because they are not connected with a church. But there has been a great change.... Wiser leaders of Christianity do not desire to monopolize the services of Christian men for the churches, but rejoice in seeing the power of religion flow out in the service of justice and mercy. Religion is less an institution and more a diffused force than ever before.

Responding to the cry for greater social awareness and action, numerous "social ministry" organizations were launched. Individual churches also began upscaling their charitable activities. But as well-meaning and progressive as this new wave of theology appeared, many felt there was little gained in helping the less fortunate if they were not directed to the Supreme Provider, Jesus Christ. "What profit it a man if he gains the whole world but loses his own soul?" they asked.

The social gospel was in contrast to the message of fundamentalist preachers like Dwight L. Moody and Billy Sunday. Robert S. Michaelson, in his study of *"The Protestant Ministry in America: 1850 to the Present,* said:

Moody preached a gospel with but one center, God's saving act in Jesus Christ, and one goal, the conversion and salvation of the sinner. All other ends were secondary.... Public morality was to be improved through saving individuals. The church was a voluntary association of the saved.

Author Sydney Ahlstrom added:

His [Moody] optimism was revealed in his confidence that individual conversions would solve every personal and social problem. Charitable works were not an end in themselves, but a means of reaching individuals with a message of redemption.

Since the early 1900s there has been a tension between the preaching of the gospel and the attempt to alleviate social dilemmas in service to God. To some degree, that debate still rages within the Church.

IMMIGRATION

In the years following the Civil War, seven million European immigrants landed at American ports. They would have a lasting impression on the Church, as respect for the Sabbath began to fade and Catholicism and Lutherean teachings gained rapid popularity.

Between 1901-1910 more than eight million foreigners immigrated to the United States. They brought with them a myriad of religious doctrines, many of which were assimilated into America's mainstream religions.

CHURCH IN TRANSITION

Professor of Sociology at Princeton University, Robert Wuthnow, in his book *The Restructuring of American Religion*, addressed the factors which transformed the Church in the years following World War II. He said, "In saying that American religion has undergone a restructing I mean to suggest that it has to some extent been remolded by the force of changes in the larger society." He pointed to the advances in technology, changes in international relationships and populations, the progress made in education, and the growth and influence of government as having an effect on the Church.

As Wuthnow suggested, the government's role in the redefining of the Church cannot be underestimated. Before World War II, the Church played a vital part in American life, but when it abdicated its responsibilities the government filled the void and acquired more and more stature in society. Since then, the courts and legislative branch of government have prohibited the Church from reassuming its prominent role.

Since the Church assumed a less visible posture, numerous changes have occurred. Wuthnow's list included a "greater room for interpretation of doctrinal creeds, self-conscious syncretism of symbolism from several of the world's religions, a more privatized form of religious expression, mixtures of social-scientific and theological reasoning, and a more universalistic style of legitimating myth."

THE JESUS PEOPLE

The Church settled into a state of comfort in the 1950s. Holding church membership was as common as carrying a social security card. Listening to three-point sermons and gospel choirs, wearing three-piece suits, and attending church potlucks were part of the weekly routine. A decade later, with the emergence of the hippy revolution and the Jesus People movement, that storybook way of life changed. Many churches were faced with what they perceived as a disruptive influence. Hippies and former drug addicts who had accepted Christ were testing the waters to see if they could find a niche in traditional churches. Some religious leaders refused to open their arms to the new converts, according to Chuck Smith's book *The Jesus People*, for they disapproved of their "simplistic mentality, the excessive emphasis on experience and feeling, and their bias against intellectual pursuits, social involvement, and human culture in general."

Smith wrote, "While some hip youth looked to Eastern mysticism, American Indian religious lore, or meditation for some kind of transcendental experience, others discovered Jesus—not in the institutional church, for organized religion held little appeal, but in the simple message of the gospel and the teachings of Christ."

Churches did not know how to respond to the "Jesus Freaks" and casually dismissed them as over-zealous misfits. As a result, the young converts fled to where they would find acceptance—to cults like the "Children of God." "It is dismaying, though not surprising," said Smith during the movement's heyday, "to hear of Jesus People who have relapsed into drugs and illicit sex. We have heard of young people reading the Bible while high on drugs and unmarried couples first praying, then sleeping together. Entire ministries, communal and other, have fallen apart because of such relapses."

CATHOLIC CHARISMATIC MOVEMENT

In the mid-1960s the Church encountered a unique episode in its history. The Pentecostal experience re-emerged within the ranks of Catholicism. The Universities of Notre Dame and Michigan became hotbeds for the Catholic Charismatic Renewal which also gave rise to a new spirit of cooperation within the Christian community. Catholics and Evangelicals began worshipping together.

Though there are still remnants of this movement and

some positive ramifications, the glory days have long since dissipated. The causes for the era's gradual decline have been debated in various circles, with varying degrees of optimism that the spirit of those days will be revisited.

THE NEW THEOLOGY

In 1933, thirty-four liberal thinkers, including John Dewey, penned a religious document: Humanist Manifesto I. The preface of the doctrinal paper revealed the group's secular ideology:

> The time has come for widespread recognition of the radical changes in religious beliefs throughout the modern world. The time is past for mere revision of traditional attitudes. Science and economic change have disrupted the old beliefs. Religions the world over are under the necessity of coming to terms with new conditions created by a vastly increased knowledge and experience.[3]

The humanists wrote openly of their antagonism toward Christendom:

> Religious humanists regard the universe as self-existing and not created.... Religious humanism considers the complete realization of human personality to be the end of man's life and seeks its development and fulfillment in the here and now. This is the explanation of the humanist's social passion.... In place of the old attitudes involved in worship and prayer the humanist finds his religious emotions expressed in a heightened sense

of personal life and in a cooperative effort to promote social well-being.[4]

Forty years after Humanist Manifesto I was composed, Humanist Manifesto II was formulated. In the preface to the second document, Paul Kurtz and Edwin H. Wilson wrote:

> As in 1933, humanists still believe that traditional theism, especially faith in the prayer-hearing God, assumed to love and care for persons, to hear and understand their prayers, and to be able to do something about them, is an unproved and outmoded faith. Salvationism, based on mere affirmation, still appears as harmful, diverting people with false hopes of heaven hereafter. Reasonable minds look to other means for survival.[5]

The credo was signed by such individuals as Ed Doerr of the Americans United for Separation of Church and State, Alan Guttmacher of Planned Parenthood, and Betty Friedan of the National Organization of Women. It addressed a variety of issues such as religion, ethics, individual rights, democracy, and more:

> We believe, however, that traditional dogmatic or authoritarian religions that place revelation, God, ritual, or creed above human needs and experience do a disservice to the human species.... But we reject those features of traditional religious morality that deny humans a full appreciation of their own potentialities and responsibilities.... Often traditional faiths encourage dependence

rather than independence, obedience rather than affirmation, fear rather than courage.... Promises of immortal salvation or fear of eternal damnation are both illusory and harmful.... Ethics is autonomous and situational, needing no theological or ideological sanction. Ethics stems from human need and interest.... We believe that intolerant attitudes, often cultivated by orthodox religions and puritanical cultures, unduly repress sexual conduct. The right to birth control, abortion and divorce should be recognized.... To enhance freedom and dignity the individual must experience a full range of civil liberties in all societies.... It also includes a recognition of an individual's right to die with dignity, euthanasia, and the right to suicide.[6]

The efforts of secular humanists have been paramount in the subtle shift in the public's perception of the Creator. In Dr. Robert A. Morey's book *Battle of the Gods*, he discussed the secular humanists' attempt to deny the historic conception of God:

What we think about God is very important, because a direct relationship exists between what people think and how they live.... If someone believes that an infinite, all-knowing, and all powerful God is holding him accountable for all his thoughts, words, and deeds, and that this God will sovereignly bring him into judgement one day, this will tend to curb his violent tendencies and dampen his lusts. If, on the other hand, he believes that no ultimate accountability or judgement will occur because God does not exist, or that God is neither omniscient nor sovereign, or that we are all god or gods, then nothing really will curb his evil ways.... The historic Christian conception of God supplied Western man with an Absolute rooted in an infinite-personal God who was both all-powerful and all-knowing. With God as an infinite absolute, it was possible to derive absolutes for every area of life.... When Western philosophies rejected the Christian conception of God, they automatically went on to deny the idea that anything or anyone was infinite. In that instant, they lost any sense of the Absolute. They viewed themselves as finite men living in a chance-caused finite universe. Nothing was infinite or absolute. Everything was relative. Truth was simply a life not yet found out.[7]

In the Garden of Eden, Satan attempted to bring God to man's level and raise man up to the level of a god. In reality, modern religions, including Secular Humanism, have engaged in a similar attack.

A SECULARIZED CHURCH

Harvard professor Harvey Cox, author of *The Secular City*, has said secularization is "the loosing of the world from religious and quasi-religious understandings of itself, the dispelling of all closed world-views, the breaking of all supernatural myths and sacred symbols." Many liberal theologians like Cox have invited and abetted the onslaught of secularism. They have viewed, said Cox, "the secularization of the world not as a massive defection from faith but rather as a further step in the historic relationship of Christianity to culture. Secularism is the 'defatalization of history.' It puts the responsibility for what happens next squarely in man's hands."

Many have also maintained that because society has been secularized, the Church must assimilate secular ways to survive. They declare traditional values and biblical interpretations as invalid, having become outdated for the modern man who dares to seize control of his individual world. Unfortunately, many churches bought the lies fostered by secularists and, consequently, allowed their sanctuaries and pulpits to become spiritually barren. Laymen began to hear more about **their** power, potential, and prowess than God's nature, authority, and will. "Attaining" and "retaining" supplanted "sharing" and "worshiping."

Author Henlee H. Barnette referred to the new theology when he said, "In too many instances the Christian faith has devolved into civic religiosity, a religion of the masses, the cult of the American way of life. This is a radical religiosity, a synthesis of patriotism, capitalism, tolerance, and affluency. God is conceived as a 'good guy' and 'fun to know,' a God to be manipulated to satisfy the hunger for peace and security."

The secularists have demoted Jesus Christ to the status of "a good man" who had characteristics worthy of being emulated; yet they deny His deity and resurrection. Many who have accepted this secularistic message still consider themselves Christians; and perhaps that is indicative of the secularists' success in polluting the gospel message. Rather than the secular humanists, some would say it was the Christian leaders of the modern era who have led the Church astray. Men like Norman Vincent Peale became prophets of comfort and prosperity to thousands, if not millions, of followers. Peale and others preached a positive thinking, self-help doctrine bordering on humanism.

With ministers and priests irresponsibly interpreting Scripture to suit the passions of their flock, it is not surprising that many Christians are theologically befuddled. The scriptural confusion brought on by secularism has served to once again cast into question the Church's authority and, sadly, its authenticity.

THE NEW AGE

Because segments of the Church were looking through glasses tinted with secularism, they were oblivious to the encroachments being made on Christianity by cults and other anti-God groups. These religions experienced success because they were able to blend their ideas with traditionally accepted beliefs. Many mystic, cultic religions failed to flourish in the United States because they could not lure believers from their sanctuaries without demanding that they discard their traditional faith. New Age leaders successfully drew followers from both Protestantism and Catholicism because they shrewdly packaged their religion in half truths and biblical trimmings.

The New Age religions teach that man has the innate potential to heighten his consciousness or spiritual awareness to the level attained by Jesus Christ. With the Holy Spirit's help, Christians strive to follow their Savior's example, whereas New Agers, independent of Divine guidance, endeavor to raise their own level of spirituality so as to become gods. This and other prominent New Age teachings have quietly infiltrated many local churches. Consequently, out of ignorance and misdirection, many churchgoers are serving a "new age" god—themselves.

THE CHURCH IN THE 1990s

Despite the assessment from analysts that the Church is in decline and inevitably facing annihilation, the fate of the Christian community remains in its own hands. The Church has the resources, a biblical mandate, and guidance from the living God at its disposal. If indeed Christianity is in decline (some delightedly claim the Church is in the midst of a membership crisis) it is a byproduct of insufficient faith, preoccupation and misdirection.

Some critics have predicted that churches in the United States are on the same path chosen by England. That country's church population forty years ago included 60 percent of its citizenry. Today, less than 4 percent are adherents to a church.

A Gallup Poll in 1988 found that three thousand American church members were leaving the church each month. Since 1976, those who consider themselves religiously unaffiliated has increased by 50 percent. Jim Castelli and George Gallup, Jr. said:

> The religiously unaffiliated are actually increasing at a faster rate than Evangelicals, those who describe themselves as 'born-again' Christians. Evangelicals actively invite others to join their church, but their proportion of the population has remained stable. In 1976, 34 percent of Americans were Evangelicals; in 1988, 33 percent were Evangelicals.... Surveys conducted throughout 1988 found that 35 percent of Americans did not belong to any church or synagogue, an all-time high. A 1988 study found that the percentage of Americans who are 'unchurched' had grown from 41 percent in 1978 to 44 percent. The study defined

the unchurched as those who are either not members of a church or synagogue or who had not attended services in the previous six months except for special religious holidays or weddings, funerals or the like.[8]

But according to Gallup and Castelli these trends are contrary to the deepening of faith in the country:

> By many measures, the unchurched are more religious than they were a decade ago. For example, 44 percent said they had made a commitment to Christ, up from 38 percent, and 72 percent say they believe Jesus is God or the Son of God, up from 64 percent. This increased religiosity among the unchurched is a good illustration of how many Americans are retaining, and even deepening, their personal faith while drifting away from active church involvement.[9]

The director of the University of Southern California's School of Religion, Robert Ellwood, speculated that Christianity has recently entered into the "final folk" stage on its way to extinction. Ellwood does not rule out the possibility, however, that Christianity will rebound. The *Los Angeles Times*, reporting the professor's theories, said:

> It was a common prediction 50 years ago that Christianity would decline in public impact, but, at least in the United States, polls and other indicators show that religious practice and beliefs still flourish, most exuberantly in the charismatic-Pentecostal churches. At the same time, main-

stream churches are suffering steady membership losses while conservative church leaders, no
matter how well their churches do, complain that
their viewpoints on abortion, pornography, school
prayer, and other moral issues are too often ignored in the public arena..... Christianity accom-
modates itself more to the non-religious side of
society. 'Modern Christians celebrate Christmas
and other holidays as both secular and religious
festivals....' 'When the social nature of the sacred
is discovered, its days are numbered and socio-
logical knowledge has replaced religious truth.'[10]

Numerous opinion makers have noted that Americans have become increasingly irritated by the infighting
between radical and conservative religionists. Not only
have theological conflicts entered public view, but also
the myriad of disagreements surrounding social issues
such as abortion, euthanasia, and homosexuality. Antagonism between religious bodies—prompted by differences in theological stances and moral convictions—is
nothing new to the United States; but at no time in history
have such disputes been so newsworthy.

The Church's efforts to fulfill God's commission of
"winning the lost" and serving as the "salt of the earth"
have certainly been disrupted by denominational dis-
unity. The most serious inhibitor, however, has stemmed
from the Church's decision to watch secularists dismantle
the nation's biblical foundation without posing an objec-
tion. Opinions, laws, and civic behavior are based more
on societal inclinations and the demands of humanistic
parties than they are the Scriptures. As society's estima-
tion of the Bible diminishes, the job of evangelism becomes all the more difficult.

An example of the lack of respect for biblical principles was reflected in another study conducted by Gallup for the Christian Broadcasting Network. The Associated Press reported on Gallup's findings:

> Nearly 80 percent of college students say religion is important in their lives but their faith has relatively little impact on their sexual behavior and attitudes, according to a new campus survey.... Nevertheless, 69 percent of the students said they do not believe premarital sex is wrong and 56 percent said they approve of living together in trial marriages. Half said they approve of the current status of abortion rights, with 9 percent of female students saying they had had an abortion and 15 percent of the males saying their partners had had one.[11]

TELEVISION EVANGELISM

The birth of Christian television was at first hailed as the panacea for an evangelistically passive Church. "The gospel will be transmitted into every household," Christian leaders promised. But when the lights and cameras came on, many Christians abdicated their witnessing obligations to television personalities wearing shiny suits and jewelry. Believers redirected their offerings from local churches to television ministries, then church participation and attendance began to decrease.

When some of these TV gurus strayed from their holy trail, they tarnished the Christian name and the message contained in their large leather Bibles. Some experienced sex scandals; others were accused of misappropriating funds and unethical fundraising tactics. The backlash came in the form of public distrust, the loss of potential converts, and damage to the legitimate Christian television industry.

SEPARATION OF CHURCH AND STATE

In 1856, Robert Baird clarified the First Amendment as it pertained to the "separation of Church and state" issue. He wrote:

> That [the First Amendment] is to say, the General Government shall not make any law for the support of any particular church, or of all the churches. But neither this, nor any other article in the Constitution of the United States, prohibits individual States from making such laws.... It (religion) is essential to the interests of men, even in this world, that they should be neither ignorant of, nor indifferent to, the existence, attributes, and providence of one Almighty God, the Ruler of the universe; and, above all, a people that believe in Christianity can never consent that the government they live under should be indifferent to its promotion, since public as well as private virtue is connected indissolubly with a proper knowledge of its claims, and as the everlasting happiness of men depends upon its cordial reception.

Secularists have attempted to reinterpret the founders' intention for the sole purpose of bridling the Church, to eradicate the influence of believers in the civic arena.

MORAL MAJORITY

It was the separation of church and state lie, the widespread immorality, the disrespect for human life, and the infringement on Christians' rights which led to the founding of the Moral Majority. Its leader, the Reverend Jerry Falwell, wielded the influence of thousands as the ranks of his organization mounted. Comprised of primarily mainstream Evangelicals, the Moral Majority was one of the Church's most promising means of fighting back, of combatting the de-Christianization of America. As in the eighteenth and nineteenth centuries, Christians began taking a stand against the secularists' agenda. Though the Moral Majority was not successful in putting prayer back in the classroom or making abortion illegal, the group did arouse the Church to action. Soon other like-minded organizations were conceived to represent the biblical position in the civic arena.

ABORTION AND THE CHURCH

The Moral Majority devoted much of its resources to the unborn's right to life, but Catholics had entered the fight to end abortion years earlier. They understood the significance lying behind the fate of the unborn.

John Whitehead, in his book *The Stealing of America*, reiterated what Catholics had been saying for many years:

> This [abortion] brings us to an important point. It is not simply that modern men hate life, but that they hate the Creator. Every person and every infant in the womb is in the image of God and possesses the resulting dignity given by the Crea-

tor. When the abortionist kills an unborn baby he is in reality killing the image of God. Although abortionists make the argument that the unborn infant is not a person, their position is, in actuality, based upon the nonexistence of any image of God or dignity of prenatal life— because of the nonexistence of God and the nonoccurrence of creation.[12]

No issue nudged the reluctant Church back into the civic arena like the controversy surrounding abortion. Robert Wuthnow wrote:

> A survey conducted in 1980...found that 72 percent of those who thought morals had been deteriorating felt religious groups should be having more political influence.... In a 1978 Gallup study, 68 percent of the evangelicals who thought abortion was never acceptable felt the churches should try to influence legislation.... In other words, the more strongly one was opposed to abortion, the more likely that person was to favor political action on the part of religious organizations.... Pretty clearly, morally conservative evangelicals wanted their churches to speak out because they figured what was said would support their own views.[13]

Sadly, not until the secularists had already won numerous battles, did religious leaders speak up.

In the 1980s, with the growth of Operation Rescue and other activist groups, many churches began speaking in behalf of the unborn; others were forced to wrestle with their positions on abortion.

Chuck Colson and other evangelical leaders have endorsed civil disobedience as a means of protesting the nation's abortion laws. "There comes a point," Colson noted, "when you have to say, 'If we really believe abortion is taking a human life created in the image of God, then we have to stand.' And if we have exhausted the political process, we have to engage in the act of civil disobedience."

When asked what the Church can do to stop the abortion holocaust, Colson suggested:

> First we must appeal to the sensibilities of people. We have to change people's minds about what is murder. The pro-life movement has been very successful in convincing 57 percent of the people that abortion is murder. So we must constantly talk about the murder of unborn children until it sinks down into the public consciousness. People must be brought to deal with the incredible schizophrenia of recognizing it as murder on the one hand, and favoring it on the other. Eventually you will get some consistency. Second, we also have to provide alternatives to abortion. We have to have crisis pregnancy centers. We must provide counseling, encouragement, practical help to pregnant women in need. Third, we need to get laws passed, but not assume laws will stop abortion. The law should be a moral teacher—and ultimately that's the importance of anti-abortion laws.[14]

SILENCING THE CHURCH

Lutheran theologian Richard Neuhaus, author of *The Naked Public Square*, contended that by a strict interpretation of separation of church and state, religious values are being excluded from the civic arena. He said, "We exclude from public discourse precisely the moral visions that are held by the great majority of the American people...."

Neuhaus wrote:

> A major problem, however, is that a public ethic cannot be reestablished unless it is informed by religiously grounded values. That is, without such an engagement of religion, it cannot be reestablished in a way that would be viewed as democratically legitimate. The reason for this is that, in sociological fact, the values of the American people are deeply rooted in religion.[15]

Neuhaus inferred, however, that there are only remnants of Christianity in the public square. He said:

> Determined secularists view these as residual inconsistencies that they have not yet got around to extirpating and that may not be worth bothering about.... From the secularist perspective it may be that the essential battles have been won and excessive zeal in pressing a final mopping-up operation might only excite further public hostility.[16]

The Church must thrust itself into the civic arena and allow its votes and voices to be heard. Christians must understand that they are involved in a spiritual battle, a war where the opposition is attempting to neutralize the gospel, believers, and Judeo-Christian values. They are attempting to silence the Church. Furthermore, they are endeavoring to divorce this society from God.

C.S. Lewis said, "A Christian society is not going to arrive until most of us really want it: and we are not going to want it until we become fully Christian." In other words, Christians must throw down the rags of apathy and expose this world to the love of Jesus Christ as it relates to every aspect of human existence, including the civic arena. Secularists, politicians, and activists must sense God's presence through the vessels which make up the Church: believers. Only then will this secular state begin the journey back to becoming a Christian nation. And with firm conviction, the Church must never again be lulled into complacency. The future of America depends on it.

A *New York Times* anti-abortion editorial in the 1870s said, "It is useless to talk of such matters with bated breath, or to seek to cover such terrible realities with the veil of a false delicacy.... From a lethargy like this it is time to rouse ourselves. The evil that is tolerated is aggressive...[so] the good...must be aggressive too." Amen!

About the Authors

Marty Pay is vice-chairman of the Southern California Constitution Education Committee and a board member of Sanctity of Human Life Ministries in the San Fernando Valley. He is the chairman of the board of the Crisis Pregnancy Center of Tehachapi, California. A prominent businessman, Pay is a highly visible pro-life, pro-family advocate. He is a frequent guest on radio and his articles have appeared in numerous publications. Pay is the former field director of California Business for Traditional Values.

Hal Donaldson is a journalism graduate of San Jose State University. He served as editor of *ON Magazine* and taught at Bethany Bible College. He is the president of ChurchCare Network, an organization that sends ministries—at no cost—to smaller churches. He has written numerous books, including *Where is the Lost Ark?, One Man's Compassion, Treasures in Heaven,* and *Ungagging the Church.*

235

Resources

Charles Sheldon's *In His Steps* was one of the largest selling books of the first half of the twentieth century. Therein, a mythical pastor exhorts his flock to ask themselves: "What would Jesus do?"

The authors have the conviction that Jesus is calling Christians to participate in the civic arena—to follow His example.

As believers reflect on this book and assess their involvement in civic affairs, they are urged to prayerfully consider what Jesus is asking of them.

The following is a partial list of publications and organizations which can provide information and opportunities for service.

Focus on the Family Citizen Magazine
Pomona, CA 91799

I'd Speak Out on the Issues: If I Only Knew What to Say
by Jane Chastain, Regal Books

Between the Lines
325 Pennsylvania Ave., SE
Washington, DC 20003

Good News Communications
2876 Mabry Rd. NE
Atlanta, GA 30319

American Family Association
P.O. Box 2440
Tupelo, MS 38803

Western Center for Law and Religious Freedom
3855 E. La Palma, No. 124
Anaheim, CA 92807

Foundation for American Christian Education
2946 25th Ave.
San Francisco, CA 94132

California Care Coalition
221 E. Walnut, No. 242
Pasadena, CA 91109

SCCEC
16628 Liggett St.
Sepulveda, CA 91343

National Right to Life
419 7th St., NE, 5th floor
Washington, DC 20004

Traditional Values Coalition
100 S. Anaheim Blvd.
Anaheim, CA 92805

Concerned Women of America
370 L'Enfant Promorade
Washington, DC 20004

Operation Rescue
9852 Katella Ave., No. 353
Anaheim, CA 92804

Christian Coalition
825 Greenbriar Circle
Chesapeake, VA 25320

NOTES

Chapter One
1. Burke, Edmund, *Selected Writings of Edmund Burke*, edited by W.J. Bate (New York: Modern Library, 1960), pp. 124-125.

Chapter Two
1. Gash, Norman, "Reflections on the Revolution," *National Review*, 14 July 1989, p. 36.
2. op. cit., Ibid., pp. 35-36.

Chapter Three
1. Cord, Robert L., *Separation of Church and State* (Grand Rapids, MI: Baker), p. xiv.
2. Timberlake, James, *Prohibition and the Progressive Movement* (Cambridge, MA: Harvard, 1963), p. 1.
3. Mowry, George, *The Twenties* (Englewood Cliffs, NJ: Prentice Hall, 1963), p. 121.
4. Engelmann, Larry, *Intemperance* (New York: Free Press, 1979), pp. 170, 172.
5. Colson, Chuck, *Born Again* (New York: Bantam, 1977), p. 66.

Chapter Four
1. Bird, Caroline, *The Invisible Scar* (NY: David Mckay, 1966), p. 160.
2. Anderson, David, *William Jennings Bryan* (Boston: Twayne, 1981), p. 190.
3. "Fossilization of Darwin's Pet," *Los Angeles Times*, "29 October 1989.
4. "Our Schools Should Teach About Religion," *USA Today*. 30 November 1989.
5. "Must Adolescenes Submit to the Chain Saw of Sex Education in the Public Schools?" *Los Angeles Times*, 27 April 1989.

Chapter Five
1. McLean, Albert F., *American Vaudeville as Ritual* (University of Kentucky Press, 1965), p. 6.
2. "Curbing Violence on TV Screens," *Contra Costa Times*, 1989.
3. "Critics Corner, *Los Angeles Times*, 21 May 1989.
4. Lennon, John, *John Lennon in His Own Words* (New York: Quick Fox, 1981), p. 59.

5. *Focus on the Family Newsletter*, 28 February 1989.
6. "Beware the Tides of March," *New York Times*, 4 March 1989.

Chapter Six
1. *On Magazine*, vol 1: no. 3, p. 16.

Chapter Seven
1. D'Antonio, William V., and Aldous, Joan, *Families and Religions* (Beverly Hills: Sage, 1983), pp. 85-86.
2. Ibid., p. 98.
3. "Gay Marriages: Make Them Legal," *New York Times*, 4 March 1989.

Chapter Eight
1. Toynbee, Arnold J., *A Study of History* (New York: Oxford University, 1947), p. 402.
2. Quoted in J.C. Willke, *Slavery and Abortion*, p. 17.
3. Ibid., p. 32.
4. Bailey, L.R., *Indian Slave Trade in the Southwest* (Los Angeles: Westernlore, 1966), pp. 25-26.
5. Quoted in Paul Marx, *The Mercy Killers*, p. 2.
6. Donohue, William A., *The Politics of the ACLU* (Transaction Books, 1985), p. 14.
7. Ibid., p. 301.
8. Ibid., p. 310

Chapter Ten
1. Quoted in Peter Collier and David Horowitz, *The Rockefellers* (New York: Holt, Rinehart and Winston, 1976), p. 3.
2. Allen, Frederick Lewis, *The Big Change* (New York: Bantam, 1965), p. 100.
3. Ibid., p. 132.
4. Bird, op cit., p. xvii.
5. Hill, Napoleon, *Think and Grow Rich* (Cleveland: Ralston Society, 1950), pp. 70, 71, 79.

Chapter Eleven
1. Allen, op cit., pp. 118-119.
2. Colson, op cit., pp. 181-182.
3. Johnson, op cit., p. 48.
4. Perret, Geoffrey, *A Country Made by War* (New York: Random

House, 1989), p. 45.

5. Allen, op. cit., p. 143.

6. Quoted in Chuck Colson, *Kingdoms in Conflict*, p. 180.

7. Fosdick, Harry E., *The Living of These Days* (New York: Harper and Brothers, 1956), p. 303.

8. Perret, op. cit., pp. 533-534.

9. Solzhenitsyn or Berman, op. cit., p. 14.

Chapter Twelve

1. Quoted in Rodger Van Allen, *American Religious Values and the Future of America* (Philadelphia: Fortress, 1978), p.16.

2. Kuiper, op. cit., p. 346.

3. *Humanist Manifesto I and II*, edited by Paul Kurtz (Buffalo, NY: Prometheus Books, 1973), pp. 7-9, 13, 15-19.

4. Ibid., pp. 8-9.

5. Ibid., p. 13.

6. Ibid., pp. 15-19.

7. Morey, Dr. Robert A., *Battle of the Gods* (Southbridge, MA: Crown, 1989), pp. 1, 2, 4, 22.

8. "Ranks of Religiously Unaffilited are Growing," *Indianapolis News*, 12 August 1989.

9. Ibid.

10. "Most Major Religions in Final 'Folk' Stage, Scholar Theorizes," *Los Angeles Times*, 18 February 1989.

11. "Christian Broadcasting Survey: Faith has Little Impact on Sex Behavior," *Contra Costa Times*.

12. Whitehead, John W., *The Stealing of America* (Westchester, IL: Crossway), p. 44.

13. Wuthnow, op. cit., pp. 202-203.

14. Ibid.

15. Neuhaus, Richard John, *The Naked Public Square* (Grand Rapids, MI: Eerdmans, 1984), p. 21.

16. Ibid., p. 25.